The Apathetic and Bored Church Member

Psychological and Theological Implications

A Research Document
from
LEAD Consultants, Inc.

The Apathetic and Bored Church Member

Psychological and Theological Implications

Dr. John S. Savage

LEAD Consultants, Inc.
P.O. Box 311
Pittsford, New York 14534

This book is dedicated to
my wife Mary Anna,
my sons
Steven and Scott,
and to my daughter
Sandra.

Preface

In mid-summer 1973, I looked through materials in a green storage cabinet and found a box of 35mm slides used in an every member canvass in the fall of 1969, Out of curiosity, I opened the box and held some slides up to my office window. A number of persons in the pictures had held important offices in the congregation, but were now inactive members. I explored more pictures and found my first observation was confirmed. What happened to these persons? How and why did they slip from among our active ranks? These questions provided the motivation and direction for this work.

I have wondered whether it was luck or providence that led me to that box and a meeting with some friends at Colgate Rochester/Bexley Hall/Crozer Theological Seminaries. At that meeting I sat next to Dr. James Ashbrook for lunch, and he informed me of the doctoral program being started in the fall. He inquired if I might be interested in becoming a part of it. I was interested and immediately began making preparations for that possibility.

After conferring with my family, parish, and denomination's ecclesiastical hierarchy, I was granted permission to return to school full time (twenty percent work in the parish). I am, therefore, grateful to my wife, Mary Anna, and my three children, Sandra, Scott and Steven, who have supported my studies, and endured, in part, an absentee husband and father. I wish to thank my parish, who felt free to release me for a year, and Bishop Joseph Yeakel, who not only served on my Dissertation Committee, but also gave the formal approval.

Gratitude goes to Dr. Edward Thornton, from the Divinity School faculty, and Dr. Harvey Resnick, from the Rochester Mental Health Center, who acted as the designing team for the research strategy. Without them, much of my planning would have gone awry.

Deep appreciation goes to the Planning and Research Committee of the Western New York Conference of the United Methodist Church. Its many suggestions, along with its formal and financial backing has meant much to me. It was through that Committee that funds were made available to support this research project.

None of the statistics and data would have been secured without the help of thirteen fellow clergypersons who did the interviews. I feel deeply indebted to them for their many hours of service and their emotional support.

Considerable thanks also goes to the four congregations who volunteered to expose themselves to this undertaking.

My undying gratitude goes to three secretaries from my parish, June Carter, Patricia Barkley and Teddie DeWeese, who typed and retyped this manuscript. Their patience and caring were of immense help. Much appreciation is also felt for the critical reading of the text by

i

Virginia Wolf, and Rev. David Roe who compiled the Reference Index. My fellow classmates are given my heartfelt thanks. They contributed much to the final structure of this work, and their questions and insights became important factors in both the design and shape which the following pages exhibit.

Finally, my deepest gratitude goes to Dr. James Ashbrook, Dr. Kenneth Cauthen, Dr. Kenneth Smith, and Bishop Joseph Yeakel, who acted as personal advisors in the creating of the original dissertation from which this document is produced. Their many hours of critical reading and reviews helped me develop this document toward a practical use.

Table of Contents

Chapter 1

Introduction

One common phenomenon in the Christian Church is the inactive and disinterested member. Both clergy and laity wrestle with this continuing problem. How can I help more of my people become active? Why do some people stay active and others drift away? What kinds of programs can I create that will attract more people? These and other questions are asked with great concern and frustration.

I discovered my problem accidentally. I was looking at old slides used in an every member canvass. Many people active when the slides were made were not active four years later. I wanted to know why. What happened? Why had some people stayed active, while others had moved into inactivity?

I felt that some form of research should be done to study the inactivity process. I wanted to find out what happens to a church member who at one time is active in the center of the church's life and two or three years later is disinterested.

Information gained from research would allow several important things to take place. First, the research could supply clues to signals given by parishioners when "moving away" from church participation. I also hoped to gain information to guide and facilitate training, enabling clergy and laity to minister more effectively in their parishes.

In addition to the original research project, I would look into existing literature for similar information. Bringing my findings into the pool of knowledge with other information could bring both insight and training skills to a problem in many liberal, mainline, conservative, and independent congregations.

STATEMENT OF THE PROBLEM

The following questions will be considered and answered in this work. What are the psychological and theological dynamics which occur in the life of a church member who is at one time active and two or three years later is inactive? Where do the affects of apathy and boredom originate? What are the behavioral differentiations that take place as a result of anxiety producing events? Does the inactive church member feel helpless or hopeless? Are there some precipitants which occur more frequently than others? Do members leaving the church blame themselves, or is there outward blame toward the institutional church? How can this differentiation be determined?

1

Limitations

The following elements characterized the research:

1. Four United Methodist congregations were used.

2. Membership in these churches ranged between 400-800.

3. The churches were similar in population, e.g., all were in suburban areas with common income ranges.

4. The same clergypersons had served in each church at least four years.

5. All churches had persons who could be categorized as active, less active, and inactive.

6. Each church provided a team consisting of the pastor and active members that screened the membership records. A minimum of fifteen names (mostly couples) were selected in each of three categories: Group A - active, Group B - less active, and Group C - inactive. The following descriptions constituted the basis for decision as to which group a person belonged:

a. Active - Group A: Those who had been active for at least three years. A person could have been active in a previous church before moving to the current church. Having pledged to the program, they had paid at least eighty percent of the pledge. They had served on one or more committees during this period. Some exceptions were made for new members, joining by affirmation of faith, who had been active for at least two years. The active parishioners attended worship at least seventy-five percent of the time.

b. Less Active - Group B: Those at one time in the "A" group were now moving into less active involvement. These persons no longer served on committees. They pledged less than in the preceeding two years. Attendance dropped by at least twenty-five percent. They were perceived as investing less emotional support to ongoing programs.

c. Inactive - Group C: This group was seen as having little or no relationship to the church. They had been "A"s previously, but now show no active participation. They had not served on committees for at least two years. They no longer pledged to the budget nor attended worship, except on special occasions like Christmas or Easter. Mailings or other informal contacts elicited little response. The inactives had been "A"s, then "B"s, but were now completely distant from their local congregation.

7. All persons interviewed were listed as members of a local church.

8. All persons contacted were adults over eighteen years of age. Their ages ranged from the early twenties to the mid-eighties.

9. Where possible, couples were interviewed together.

10. The fact that clergy served as interviewers and that the churches were suburban United Methodist limited the generalizations that could be made from the data gathered.

11. A committee of active church members chose these persons. None of the churches exhausted their lists; therefore, it would be possible to have selected others who may have had similar or quite different responses.

Length of Investigation

This project started in September of 1973 and ended in July 1974. The actual interviewing took place between May 20th and July 1st.

THEORETICAL FRAMEWORK

The theoretical framework of the project is derived primarily from the fields of psychology, psychiatry, and theology and is divided into two sections. The first is an investigation and definition of terms. The second part will delineate basic assumptions and hypotheses.

As a result of studying the psychodynamic movement of an individual from active to inactive status in the life of the church, I have developed an elaborate scheme called the "Anxiety-Anger Complex" (see page 4).

Anxiety

A basic assumption is that movement away from active church involvement is triggered by some kind of initial anxiety. Therefore, anxiety is a word of crucial importance to the basic understanding of this work.

Anxiety is the affect (feeling) which is produced by an arousal period of short or long duration when persons feel they are knocked off their equilibrium (emotional, psychical, or rational balance).[2] Anxiety is a feeling of loss of a comfortable state. Schmale claims that anxiety is "the first psychic awareness of discomfort and probably remains throughout life the first and immediate reaction to the perception of psychic tension in any situation."[3] In terms of what is felt, anxiety may range from vague feelings of uneasiness, restlessness, and foreboding to

3

Anxiety—Anger Complex

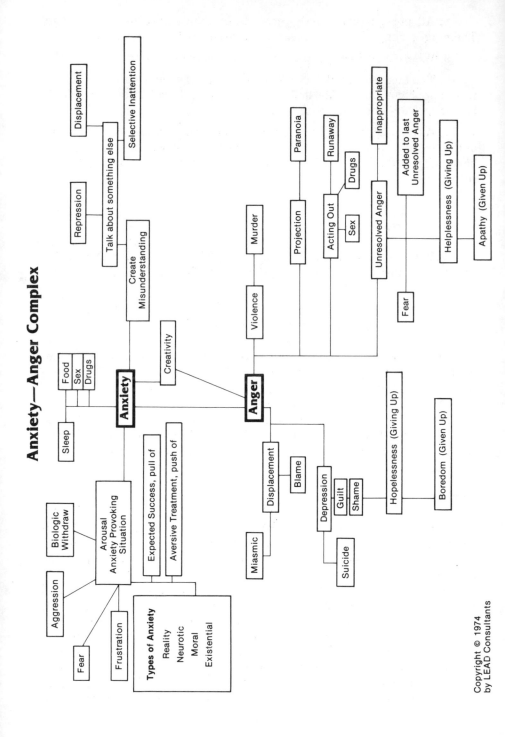

4

specifically identified fears, which may be realistic to varying degrees or may be totally unrealistic (phobias or delusions).[4]

Four types of anxiety can be distinguished:

1. *Reality:* Events occuring in one's own personal history producing pain or a sense of disequilibrium. These events are oriented in reality and do not have delusionary components.

2. *Neurotic:* Thought patterns producing feelings not based on historical events. They are delusionary in character and are free-floating with little or no concrete ties to reality events.

3. *Moral:* This form of anxiety is one in which an individual finds conflict or dilemmatic perceptions between two kinds of behavior. It is seen as knowing at a cognitive level what is expected of him or her, while doing in behavior the opposite.

4. *Existential:* Tillich is one of the authors of this descriptive form of anxiety. He states, "The first assertion about the nature of anxiety is this: anxiety is the state in which a being is aware of its possible nonbeing."[5] He further claims that anxiety is finitude, experienced as one's own finitude. In other words, it is the natural anxiety of man as man, and the anxiety of nonbeing as the awareness of one's finitude as finitude. It is that feeling brought up by the thought that some day you may not exist, and that even if you do exist, your life may be utterly meaningless.

Each of the above anxieties, or a combination of them, is found in persons moving to inactivity. Anxiety will be considered in detail later in this work.

Anger

Etymologically, the English word "anger" comes from the old Norse word "angre" which means affliction (Latin: *ad-fligere* = to strike at). In most languages, including German and Spanish, anger is a well-delimited concept and response to an offending stimulus. These languages do not use hostility, aggression, or rage to simply mean anger. Essentially, the term confers uneasiness, displeasure, and resentment.[6]

Sterns, in his book *Anger: Physiology, Psychology, Pathology,* states that "Anger may be best described as a combination of uneasiness, discomfort, tenseness, resentment (which is a response to selective stimuli), and frustration."[7]

5

Anger is the response to anxiety occurring when a person feels comfort is being taken away. I speak here of events which make for increased conflict and which arouse aggressive responses directed toward the environment.

Anger is always object-directed.[8] Anger attempts to get rid of objects or situations producing anxiety.

Anger is a means of returning to a comfortable state. Anger attacks the object or event which has caused the person to become uncomfortable, tense or uneasy. Attacking the intrusion brings the hope that anxiety will go away.

Additional Concepts

Four other terms need to be defined: helplessness and hopelessness, apathy and boredom.

Helplessness is the affect felt when an individual perceives there is no help from outside of the self. It is the feeling of losing the loved object. One gives up on any stimuli which might extricate one from a given problem. It is the response to object loss, real or fantasied, in which a person feels that he or she cannot function without the object present.

Helplessness precipitates apathy. It is giving-up a relationship, either human or material. In short, it is the awareness there is nothing outside of the self that can provide help; therefore, one is helpless.

Helplessness is felt by a parishioner moving away from an active church relationship. This feeling can be detected in the words, "It doesn't matter what I say; they will do what they want anyway."

The antithesis of helplessness is hopelessness. Hopelessness is the feeling there is no resource inside of the self to solve a problem. As helplessness is the feeling there is nothing outside of self that can help, so hopelessness is the feeling that there is nothing inside of self that can bring strength. The feeling of shame commonly precedes hopelessness in the response to some stress or anxiety.[9]

Engel comments regarding hopelessness:

The anlage of hopelessness . . . is found in the primal depression-withdrawal indicative of the fact that no help is possible and that exhaustion threatens. [10]

Two concepts emerge from the affects of helplessness and hopelessness: helplessness is the precipitant to apathy and hopelessness is the precipitant to boredom.

Sullivan claims that:

Apathy is a curious state; as nearly as I can discover, it is a way used to survive defeats without material damage, although if it endures too long, one is damaged by the passage of time. Apathy seems to me to be a miracle of protection by which personality in utter fiasco rests until it can do something else.[11]

Apathy is a form of survival when everything else seems lost. It is the feeling of "having given-up." Apathy can be described as a survival activity when the individual is under too much stress, anxiety, anger or conflict. It allows a condition through which survival can take place, even if it means isolation.

Having understood apathy as necessary for survival under difficult conditions, it can also be seen from a more negative vantage point.

In the apathetic church member, the act of isolation produces its own special effects. There is the loss of contact with friends and institutional relationships. There is the sense of meaninglessness and a denying of threatening feelings. When this occurs, there is what Tillich calls the "threat of nothingness,"[12] i.e., the possibility that all may be lost. The person senses protection from destructive feelings, while also feeling exiled from the human community. Therefore, apathy produces two different sets of responses, each effecting the other.

Boredom is the state occurring when an individual has given-up the possibility that there is strength within the self to bring about a change in the person's condition. The bored person is self-blame directed and sees his or her relationship to the world as you're OK, but I'm not OK.

Bored persons are individuals who have turned their anger inward. In its extreme form they come to realize there is nothing they can do, no power they can exercise, no internal resource available and no way of altering the external condition through internal contrivance or manipulation. They have come to be without hope. They are utterly bored and have given-up hope for their future. They have turned to the wall and found no way out. Therefore, the implications resulting from bored persons becoming distant from the church are immense.

Assumptions

An assumption can neither be verified nor denied. My assumptions take on the following form:

1. Research methods used are valid forms of gathering the data.
2. The sample size is adequate to provide sufficient and reliable information.
3. What one interviewer does in the interviewing process is consistent with other interviewers' responses.
4. The Chi-square test for significance is adequate for statistical purposes.

7

A hypothesis defines that which the research tests and therefore will either be supported or not supported by the data. The hypotheses are as follows:

1. Persons who are active, less active, and inactive in the church will agree to be interviewed.
2. In moving from active to inactive involvement in the church, the stages of a person's withdrawal can be described.
3. Movement starts from a precipitating event which produces anxiety and anger and culminates in either boredom or apathy.
4. Specific psychodynamics effect whether one moves from an active to inactive status. These include unresolved anger, frustration, powerlessness, and the denying of one's feelings.
5. The blame orientation of an active, less active, and inactive church member can be described.
6. Age, occupation, and educational level are important factors in the dropout motif, but are not the sole qualifiers.
7. The institutional structure of the church has a direct effect upon the behavior of persons who move from an active to inactive status.

DESIGN OF THE INVESTIGATION

A personal interview was the mode for gathering data. The options of my doing the interviews or having others help were considered. After weighing the effects, other clergypersons were enlisted in the data gathering procedure. The effect of my doing all the interviews had built-in biases that would be skewed toward my own personal interests.

The interview was open-ended, and, therefore, the interviewer helped the interviewees to associate freely to basic questions and then followed the lead of that content. This was a critical factor in this study because it allows the interviewer to put data together which is not necessarily seen by the person interviewed. The interview model was designed from psychiatric interview procedures.

The design team, having agreed that the home interview would be the primary mode of operation, also considered the possible use of the personal interview over the phone. This became a back-up system for securing data from persons in the "B" and "C" categories of the church populations. The personal telephone call was made to only those who had not returned their cards. There was, therefore, an attempt to contact all persons in the "B" and "C" groups. It was anticipated that there would be some differences in the population between those who chose to return their cards for an interview and those who refused to do so. The response of these people can be seen in Chapter 3.

The interview on the phone lasted ten to twenty minutes, while the home interview lasted at least fifty minutes, and, in some cases, went to two hours (frequently the extended time was spent over cake and coffee, and important feelings were shared in that "informal" time).

In summary, home and phone interviews were utilized, with the personal home interview being the more effective.

The Population

I selected four suburban type United Methodist Churches with memberships from 400 to 800. The churches are located in different geographical locations within the boundaries of the Western New York Conference of the United Methodist Church. These churches were chosen because they had similar populations and financial diversity, the predominant incomes being between $10,000 and $20,000 per family. The population included blue collar and business professions.

Married couples were chosen whenever possible. Singles, divorced, separated, widow(ed), and elderly were also a part of the sample.

Three of the four churches, Christ View, Fairport, and Orchard Park, made formal agreements with their administrative boards to have this program accomplished in their parishes. (There is an unwritten rule in the Western New York Conference that church membership rolls are the private property of the local church and should not be given out to any solicitors, i.e., a research group, without formal consent.) It should be pointed out that Epworth United Methodist Church did not make that request and had the least number of respondents.

Upon receiving the names in each of the categories, a letter was written (personally typed on an automatic typewriter) explaining the purpose of the research and asking for their help. A stamped envelope was enclosed along with a return card which was to be checked yes or no to the interview, their name, address, and phone number (see appendix for samples). The letters were sent out on stationery provided by L.E.A.D. Consultants, [13] an independent religious consulting agency of which I am president.

The interviewers were selected from the pastoral list of the Western New York Conference of the United Methodist Church. I selected fifty clergypersons, using the following criteria: (1) personally known, (2) exhibited values of caring and warmth, (3) interested in a calling ministry, (4) some training in counseling.

The training day ran from 9:00 AM to 4:00 PM and consisted of a number of activities which would acquaint the interviewers with the basic skills and knowledge that they would need. An outlined description of the training can be seen in the appendix.

The group worked in sub-groups of six during the entire day. (I find six to be an excellent working number, since groupings of one, two, three or six can be utilized.) At the onset, there were several exercises to sensitize the group to their own feelings of what it is like to be in the interviewer-interviewee positions. In this training, I follow two basic assumptions: (1) the interviewee will be more frightened and anxious than the interviewer, since the interviewer has a better idea of what is going to happen (2) the interviewers need to be in touch with their own feelings to enable them to be more sensitive to the interviewees' feelings.

There was also an extensive discussion of the Anxiety-Anger Complex (see Chapter 3), including the use of anxiety, anger, helplessness, hopelessness, boredom, and apathy.

Following this discussion, a period of time was spent on developing listening skills: paraphrasing, checking for feelings, questioning, and clarifying. These skills are used extensively in the interview process and become important in listening to another person. Skill training was provided through role playing, where each member of a team of three took the interview-interviewer role, while a third party observed and critiqued what had taken place.

Since the interviewers had the responsibility of making their own appointments, a brief phone call role play was also created and practiced.

A final section of the training event informed the interviewers in matters of policy, administrative procedures, and the use of the data gathering tool.

Extraordinary enthusiasm was created in the training event, and several Buffalo ministers volunteered to drive to the Fairport and Christ View Churches (seventy miles away) to help cover the calls needed in those parishes.

Each minister had from one to six interviews to make, depending upon his or her location.

10

Required Data

The basic premise upon which this research project was conceived is that persons move through a series of stages when going from active to inactive participation in the church. Necessary data required for such an investigation should provide methods for tracing those events which produced anxiety and anger and provided impetus for movement away from a center-core relationship. Investigation into past and present activity levels in the church and the events occurring around them provided handles upon which I could hang inferences. Areas of investigation were: conflict, the way conflict was handled, its resolution or lack of resolution, encounters with mates and other members of the family, issues over finance, theology, education, and meaningless work in the church.

The most difficult to obtain, yet most important information came from the impression of the interviewer about the helpless-hopeless characteristics of the interviewee. Because these two feelings lead to apathy and boredom, it was important to look for these characteristics. An analysis of the content enabled such a distinction to be made.

A written statement was required of each interviewer regarding the helpless-hopeless characteristics. In most cases of the helpless-hopeless prone person, the interviewer was able to note signals which helped diagnose the track (apathetic or bored) a person was taking. These signals fall into two general categories. The apathetic person tends to be more institutional-blame biased, while the bored person is personal-blame biased. This means that words, e.g., "I don't like the minister's sermons," "It's no use telling them anything; they won't listen," "I don't like the way he runs the meeting," imply movement toward institutional-blame and lead the interviewer toward the assumption of an apathetic (helpless) condition. Responses from persons saying, "I am at fault," "I don't feel as close to the people as I used to," "I have been away from the church for so long that I feel guilty about going back," are personal-blame biased and indicate a parishioner is feeling hopeless and on the way to boredom.

In many cases, it was not possible to differentiate between the helpless or hopeless patterns. When this occurred, it was concluded that the interviewee was not strongly prone to either direction. A thorough discussion of these conditions is considered in Chapters 3 and 4.

The Interview Check List

All statistical information was gathered through this instrument. The check list (see appendix) was divided into six major sections: fixed data, precipitants, living situation, religious status, and personal religious events.

NOTES

[1] Earl D. D. Brewer and Associates, *Protestant Parish* (Atlanta: Communicative Arts Press, 1967); see also Thomas C. Campbell and Yoshio Fukuyama, *The Fragmented Layman* (Philadelphia: United Church Press, 1970). Both are excellent examples of works which show the dropout problem.

[2] Albert Bandura, *Aggression: A Social Learning Analysis* (Englewood Cliffs, N.J.: Prentice Hall, 1973), p. 54.

[3] Arthur H. Schmale, Jr., "A Genetic View of Affects," *The Psychoanalytical Study of the Child*, Vol. XIX (1964), p. 290.

[4] George L. Engel, *Psychological Development in Health and Disease* (Philadelphia: W. B. Saunders Company, 1962), p. 168.

[5] Paul Tillich, *The Courage To Be* (New Haven: Yale University Press, 1956), p. 35.

[6] Frederic R. Stern, *Anger, Psychology, Physiology, Pathology* (Springfield: Charles C. Thomas, 1972), p. 5.

[7] Stern, *Anger*, p. 6.

[8] From a personal interview (taped) with Dr. Arthur H. Schmale, Jr. of the University of Rochester School of Medicine, February, 1974.

[9] Engel, *Psychological Development*, p. 175.

[10] Engel, *Psychological Development*, p. 175.

[11] Harvey Stack Sullivan, *The Psychiatric Interview* (New York: W. W. Horton and Co., Inc., 1970), pp. 184-185.

[12] Tillich, *Courage*, p. 37.

[13] L.E.A.D. Consultants, P.O. Box 311, Pittsford, N.Y. 14534. L.E.A.D. stands for Leadership, Education and Development; made up of some sixty consultants from many denominations who have pooled their talents to help the local church.

Chapter 2

Resume of Related Research and Professional Literature

Literature relating to this project covers such areas as psychology, theology, sociology, and psychiatry. I dipped into that sea of knowledge and pulled a few buckets from those vast resources. I have been selective in what I have chosen in order to illuminate the issues presented in this book.

SOCIOLOGICAL LITERATURE ON CHURCH INVOLVEMENT

In recent years there has been a large decrease in church involvement within many of the major denominations. A project of the Western New York Conference of the United Methodist Church documented a membership decrease of 83,293 in 1965 to 81,870 in 1974. In 1969 the Western New York Conference and the New York Conference of the Evangelical United Brethren Church merged and added 3,486 members. An additional 1,961 were added in 1971 when the Erie Pennsylvania Conference of the EUB Church also joined the Western New York Conference. A total of 5,447 members joined in that period, yet a net loss of 1,723 or a gross loss of 7,170 was observed.

Major losses occurred in the educational program. Youth attendance at church school dropped from 11,263 to 6,543 or 58%. Total enrollment for all ages in the church school dropped from 52,507 to 32,937 or a 62% decrease in a ten year period. [1]

These figures confirm the loss of members, yet do not show the number of persons who have become inactive and remain within the membership numbers quoted. In the four churches in my study, it was found that nearly 33% of each congregation's membership was in the inactive (C) category.

This drop in attendance and membership is reflected in other studies. In 1967 George Gallup stated that he conducted a survey which asked persons, "At the present time do you think religion as a whole is increasing its influence on American life, or losing its influence?" People responded as follows: in 1957, 69% said it was increasing; in 1967, 23% agreed; in 1957, 14% said it was losing influence; in 1967, 57% said loss was more evident. [2] The group of persons who seem to note that the loss was greater is from the 21-29 year age group, where 63% said religion was losing influence; for those over 50 it was 53%.

There is general agreement that church attendance reached a peak in 1958 and has been on the decline since. [3] In 1958 average attendance peaked with 49% of the population going to worship on any given

Sunday. By 1966 it had dropped to 44% and in 1972 to 40%.[4] Within Protestantism attendance has dropped from 38% (1966)[5] to 36% (1972).[6] Jacquet, the editor or the *Yearbook of American and Canadian Churches 1974*, points out that worship attendance figures were the same for 1971 and 1972. This leveling off had not occurred since 1958.[7] These latest figures may represent a possible shift in religious interest in our country.

Douglas W. Johnson and George W. Cornell, co-authors of *Punctured Preconceptions*, claim that people have lost interest because of a shift of priorities. (The authors do not say why the shift occurred). The authors state:

> Clergymen perpetuate an idea that apathy and dropouts result from the church having become unimportant in modern society. Both in the United States and Canada, clergymen see this as the main cause of people losing interest. But in neither country do lay people buy that line at all. They put it down as a seventh-rate factor, compared to the clergy's estimate of it as No. 1. However, while the laity consider the church important they imply that the clergy's version of it is not their kind of church and that what turns the people off is not the church's unimportance, but the pressure of time and other more compelling interests.
>
> ... Next in line, they listed loss of confidence in the church and its failure to offer an appealing program, meaning that it was not meeting their personal needs for dealing with the problems of life and so inclining them to invest their available time and energies elsewhere.[8]

Other reasons for decline can be seen from the age spread. Church participation changes along age lines. For example, less participation is experienced by the 20-34 group than any other single fourteen year age block across the life span. Even those of 65 years and over constitute a larger proportion of the active church population than those previously mentioned. The sub-age group of 30-35 is the lowest point in the life cycle for church activities.[9] This fact by Argyle is, in part, affirmed by Campbell and Fukuyama in their book, *The Fragmented Layman*.[10] The authors point out that the 20-35 year old group have only a 29% participation in organizational involvement, by far the lowest of any age group (example: 35-49 is 53%). While these studies of Argyle and Campbell/Fukuyama were conducted nearly fifteen years apart, conclusions remain the same. Pressey and Kuhlen's, *Psychological Development Through the Life Span*, purports the following reason why that age group had less involvement:

> The thirties—the low point in the age profile of religious observance—probably introduce three other factors: (1) the pressure for job success, an interest that likely has a pervasive effect upon many urban behavior patterns; (2) the demand on time of young children in the home; and (3) the desire to limit the family size through birth control, a point emphasized by experienced priests in the parish. This third factor is important because the church teaches that the

14

Catholic cannot practice birth control and also receive the sacraments. Here, then, is a rather specific conflict between purposes—and church observance suffers.[11]

Fichter reflects on the same low involvement in the 20-35 year age span in his work with the Roman Catholic Church, done in 1952.[12]

Not all denominations or sects within the church are losing members. A massive study of U.S. church membership by the Glenmary Research Center,[13] a Roman Catholic agency, in cooperation with the National Council of Churches and the Lutheran Church, Missouri Synod, found that certain denominations are growing quite rapidly, while others are declining or just holding their own. When the population growth is considered, the Catholics in the last two or three years seem to have arrived at zero growth.

The "liberal" churches—those that have identified most strongly with social activism—are suffering massive defections in favor of more orthodox or Bible centered denominations. For example, the United Presbyterian Church which made a $10,000 contribution to Angela Davis under the ambiguous heading, "Marin County Legal Defense Fund," has, according to its conservative lay committee, lost 350,000 members and $6.7 million in donations to the General Assembly during the past five years.

Among the branches of Lutheranism, the Missouri Synod, which is counted as the most conservative, grew 49% in the past twenty years, while the U.S. population increased 35%. The most liberal group, Lutheran Church in America, grew only 21%.

Southern Baptists, who are traditional, increased their numbers 45%, while the fundamentalist Pentecostals and Seventh Day Adventists rose 75%. The Mormons also had considerable growth as they nearly doubled their membership in that same period of time, while the Church of God rose 120%.

I am aware that this work might not have been written had it not been for the interest in my own denomination's loss of membership. If all were going well, with membership on the increase, the questions raised in this work probably never would have been asked. As a result of loss of membership, I was drawn to look more seriously at those problems. Loss, therefore, has become the mother of inquiry.

STUDIES ON ANXIETY

Psychological and Psychiatric Literature on Anxiety

"The presence of anxiety is much worse than its absence."[14] This statement by Harry Stack Sullivan succinctly states the essence of anxiety; none of us want it, but all of us have it. There is no conceivable circumstance in which anyone would desire it. In other words, there is no series of "useful" attacks of anxiety in therapy or outside of therapy that anyone might seek. "This is, in a good many ways, rather startling," says Sullivan, "particularly when one compares anxiety with fear. While fear has many of the same characteristics, it may actually be sought out as an experience . . ." [15] Sullivan goes on to illustrate the fact the people who ride on roller coasters pay money to be afraid, but no one will ever pay money for anxiety in its own right. The reason for this is that no one wants to experience it. Sullivan also points out that the only other experience—that of loneliness—is in this special class of being totally unwanted. Because anxiety is so unwanted, the individual engages in a variety of behaviors to provide a release from the uncomfortable feelings. The experience of anxiety is a signaling device, a sign that something ought to be different at once.

One of the complications of studying anxiety is that anxiety is considered to be a subject variable, but rarely the subject itself. The reason for this is one cannot observe anxiety. "One can observe only trembling, perspiring, and other external manifestations of anxiety. For research purposes then, anxiety and many other subject variables must be translated into measurable response variables." [16]

In my research I attempted to assess the anxiety level of those persons being interviewed. I made the assumption that one can observe the anxiety level of another human simply by observing physiological and verbal behaviors.

A large number of studies have shown anxiety and its effects. Thurston's Personality Schedule [17] measured anxiety neuroticism in thirty-six college students. Mowrer and Solomn's experiment on avoidance describes a little boy who became anxious and ran into his house every time he saw a dog. Their hypothesis was that anxiety can be conditioned, or deliberately brought about, and then, by changing the behavior, evaded. [18] They experimented with both rats and dogs to illustrate the ability of conditioning these animals. Within a short time (ten trials), the animals avoided a setting (shock producing) by moving to another part of their cages before the predetermined shock. This study suggests that persons also may avoid anxiety-evoking experiences.

In 1969, the Royal Medico-Psychological Association, in cooperation with the World Psychiatric Association, held a world conference on the problems of anxiety. [19] Among the twenty-eight scientific papers given, a study by Murray Parkes, of the Tavistock Institute, on "Separation Anxiety: An Aspect of the Search for a Lost Object," [20] relates to this research. One of the key issues suspected in the actions of a church member's moving away from deep involvement with the local church is the considerable amount of grief and loss. Parkes points out that the grief accompanying loss of friends, institutions, and mates (the loss is obviously not of the same intensity) causes a specific human behavior. That behavior is to strike back (anger) at the abandoning or rejecting object. The striking back has a multiple effect. On the one hand, it produces distance and rejection; on the other hand, it allows two persons (person-institution) to react to each other and to find each other again. Another researcher, John Bowlby, found that the crying and searching out of each other helps the separated parties to find each other, and protesting, according to Bowlby, punishes all concerned with the loss and makes it less likely that it will occur again.[21]

Insight from this kind of research made me aware of the reluctance of persons in a local congregation to take part in ecumenical ventures with other denominations. I found this true when three churches in Henrietta, New York, tried for three summers to get their congregations to worship together. This was done by moving each month to a different church, usually with the pastors staggering vacations so they would not be preaching in their own churches. The result was a very strong resistance from the parishioners to worship in the "other churches."

Douglas and Bloomfield found that, compared with controls, the incidence of nightmares was significantly raised in six year old children who had been separated from mother for a period of four weeks or longer before their sixth birthday. For 123 children who had spent four weeks or longer in hospitals, the incidence of nightmares was nearly doubled (34.4% against 15.5%). For those who had been with friends, the incidence was also significantly raised. On the other hand, no raised incidence was found in a group of children who, although separated from mother, had remained in their own homes. These findings suggest that the stranger the surroundings in which a separated child finds himself or herself, the more anxiety is provoked in him or her, a conclusion supported by other studies.[22]

It may first appear extreme to equate this child study with church attendance. I infer that the child's anxiety in being separated from important objects is a feeling we carry all through our lives. To leave the object of our affection, as in the case of one's local church, brings back that feeling. This understanding is supported by Arthur Schmale when looking at the genetic history of the feeling of anxiety:

> Anxiety is postulated to reflect the earliest psychic awareness of biological disequilibrium and is herein considered to be the undifferentiated primal prototype from which all the other affects are derived. Anxiety, then, is the first psychic awareness of discomfort, and probably remains through life the first and immediate reaction to the perception of psychic tension in any situation.[23]

The above views imply that if a person is separated from love objects, anxiety follows. If anxiety is great, the person will remove himself or herself from that situation in order to reduce the anxiety, and the state of peace or equilibrium occurs again.

In *Theories of Anxiety,*[24] Freud described anxiety as a process in which the entire mental apparatus was being overwhelmed or threatened with excessive stimulation.

Sullivan and Schachtel conceived anxiety as being fundamentally a tensional phenomenon, but for them it emerges primarily in an interpersonal context and is saturated with social meaning. Learning theorists define anxiety as a sub-type of fear. They understand this fear to be a learned drive, that is, a disruption in the organism's homeostasis finally related to the occurrence of painful stimuli. Physiologically oriented theorists regard anxiety as an effect, the cause of which is to be found in environmental stimuli.[25]

Heidegger, in his analysis of the ontological dimensions of human living, understands anxiety as an affective disposition that expresses the individual's relatedness to a world that has lost its meaning. This philosopher sees anxiety in terms of man's reluctance to come to grips with the actuality and inevitability of one's death.[26]

Kurt Goldstein developed a holistic approach to anxiety, pulling together the work of other theorists. He found that anxiety is required for growth. Actuality grows through the use of anxiety-provoking situations. As a temporal phenomenon, not a spatial one, anxiety inevitably accompanies development. The capacity to meet anxiety is, for this theorist, the meaning of courage. Courage is the moment in the process through which both the organism and the world are continually transformed by their encounter and resolution. Courage is the overcoming of the shock of an anxiety situation which allows a person to enjoy the fruits of coming to terms with the environment, and the satisfaction experienced when one has mastered a segment of the world, which outweighs the anxiety endured.[27]

The following illustration points out Goldstein's theory.

Let us assume for a moment that a man is taking a canoe downstream. By skillful balance, by holding back his canoe at certain moments, by choosing the most likely channel and using the current where he can, he achieves his purpose and remains alive and comfortable. He encounters sharp turns, overhanging branches and threatening rapids, but by skillful adaptive steering and paddling, he passes them safely. As long as he feels that he is in control of the boat in the water, his anxiety level will remain low, for his confidence will ensure his comfort. When, however, he meets some threatening situation which he encounters anew, his anxiety will rise to assure him that every cell in his body will come to bear upon the problem.

The above illustration speaks of the person whom we shall assume has a relatively healthy and intact ego, one whose "elasticity" is not greatly reduced by scars and weaknesses. Such an ego will have established relationships with love objects by which it may be deeply involved in its work and play and, therefore, find much satisfaction in what he does. With such an ego a person will have learned to channel aggressiveness in the least harmful direction and toward the universe of love objects.

Karl Menninger points out that even the most healthy-minded individual has to make choices and resort to expedience. Everyone has limits of tolerance in unexpected disturbing encounters, hard-to-bear disappointments, and unconsolable griefs.[28] As John Cowper Powys says, "Even the toughest and strongest among us may be sent howling . . .,"[29] when placed in a setting of high anxiety.

Anxiety produces "energy" that can be guided to creativity. Seward Hiltner and Karl Menninger, in *Constructive Aspect of Anxiety*, deal with the creative use of anxiety. When the emphasis is on the signal function of anxiety (the alarm system), then anxiety is not properly understood.

An alarm clock can be set to wake a person at a certain time, but the ringing of its bell, whether it be loud or soft, would not tell the person what to do or where to go when he or she gets up. One person can start his or her day by saying the morning prayers or by getting ready to perform a deed for a neighbor, water the flowers, or write a letter; another person may get up to set off a bomb that might destroy a church or a place of recreation and injure or kill hundreds of persons. In other words, anxiety is only the alarm; it is not the dictator of what the alarm is to do.

This leads us into the theological and philosophical dimensions of anxiety.

Theological Literature on Anxiety

The following statement suggests a richness and adultness in response to the anxiety of the world. Let us, ". . . join that pious woman of old who, amidst the firm tradition of Moses, Jesus, and Mohammed, was able to raise her voice and say, 'I love the Lord for what He is, not out of any fear of His punishment nor in expectation of any reward.' "[30]

Soren Kierkegaard, Reinhold Niebuhr and Paul Tillich approach anxiety differently. Kierkegaard says that "Anxiety is an expression for the perfection (making valid) of human nature." Niebuhr claims that "Anxiety is the precondition of sin," while Tillich states, "Anxiety is the existential awareness of nonbeing."

A more detailed discussion of these men may make the above statements more understandable.

Kierkegaard. The first modern theologian to deal with anxiety was Kierkegaard, commonly known as the "father of modern existentialism."[31] He began his studies by raising questions about sin.[32] Sin is what separates man from God, and, therefore, what also separates him from becoming what he ought to become. For him, sin is neither evil deeds done by a few wicked persons nor naughty ones done by everybody. If sin is "talked about as a sickness, an abnormality, a poison, a disharmony," it has already been subverted.[33]

Kierkegaard addressed himself to several questions: How does sin get started? What is the prototype of sin? What is the original sin? In his words, "The first sin is a determinant of quality, the first sin is *the* sin."[34] The first sin—this prototypical sin—comes through anxiety. Anxiety is recognition of "the reality of freedom as possibility anterior to possibility."[35] In describing this confrontation with the "possibility anterior to possibility," Kierkegaard spoke of an immense "abyss" and the "dizziness" a person experiences by looking into the "abyss" of possibility. Freedom and anxiety are two sides of the same coin; to look seriously at freedom is to confront the infinity of possibility, "which does not tempt like a definite choice, but alarms and fascinates."[36] It is the quality of alarm and fascination that make one dizzy. It is the perception that there are so many choices, as well as the belief that one is free to make them, that makes the "abyss" so deep and threatening. Anxiety, then, is the feeling we get when we look into that "abyss" and find that we are not able to cope with the alternatives. If, however, we can succeed in denying that the possibilities exist or that we do not have to be responsible for our decisions, the feelings will be less intense. In other words, we back off from the "abyss," particularly if we use freedom wrongly. For to keep looking into the possibilities of our behavior is to admit that there is more pain than we would like to consider. Pain is a temptation to retreat, and we frequently yield to the temptation.

Where, then, lies the problem? The fault is the self's inability to sustain the pain of the dizziness, not the anxiety itself. Another way of studying this problem is to examine the forces that prevent the self from confronting the dizziness, and instead permit it to retreat.

Since anxiety is the painful dizziness in the face of the "abyss" of possibility, it follows that if there is no freedom, there can be no sin. From Kierkegaard's point of view, if there were no capacity for anxiety, there would be no capacity for creativity.

For both Kierkegaard and Freud, anxiety functions as a signal when danger is confronted or as a prod to action. For them anxiety is neither constructive nor destructive. Anxiety serves a constructive function; that is, persons possess the signaling or prodding apparatus and that, in and of itself, is constructive. It is the response to that prod which allows us to be creative or destructive. Kierkegaard states that anxiety's function in human life is to compel us to accept ourselves as spirit, as well as nature; that is, as responsible, imaginative, creative and free beings who cannot pretend that we live as animals do, even though we are animals.[37] As the capacity for feeling the dizziness, anxiety is our uniquely human possession, for without it we would not be imaginative. Our sin is that we retreat from the potential of possibility, for that is always a painful gaze into the "abyss,"

Niebuhr. Kierkegaard's and Niebuhr's views about anxiety are almost identical. Niebuhr's concern about anxiety emerges out of his consideration of sin. Sin is the failure to accept one's freedom and the responsibility that goes with that failure. Sin takes two basic forms: pride and sensuality. In pride one acts as if one had no limits. In sensuality one retreats from the responsibility that accompanies freedom.

When anxious, a person is tempted to sin. He or she sets himself or herself above one's proper limits (pride) or denies one's spiritual nature by sinking back into unlimited devotion to limited values, which Niebuhr construes as sensuality.[38]

Niebuhr also speaks to the issue of sin and freedom by noting that the more freedom a person has, the more chances there are for sin; but also, the greater the chance to be responsible and creative. Niebuhr argues that the most dangerous oar-resters are the good people, the free people, the moral people, the healthy people. They find their freedom leads them into the sin of pride, resulting, he says, in damage greater than in the case of the less good, the less free, the less moral, the less healthy. "The better or freer or healthier a man is, the more it behooves him to have enough uneasiness so as not to become proud."[39]

Niebuhr states that persons have a great amount of freedom and can act responsibly. A question arises: does a person restricted by emotional paralysis have the freedom to act on one's own behalf? Niebuhr fails to consider the possibility of the mentally disturbed person. He shows little interest in therapy as a means of dealing with the anxiety state. He is inclined to believe that in these severe states, people experience enough self-transcendence to comprehend their condition. Niebuhr does not take seriously pathological conditions produced, not because they made some error in choice in the midst of their freedom, but because of compulsions developed through prior experience.

Central to our discussion, however, is that both Niebuhr and Kierkegaard see anxiety in similar ways. For both, anxiety is not the problem, but rather the resulting behavior.

The issue of anxiety and its resulting behavior serves as a central focus for the next chapter. Why is it, given the same anxiety-provoking situation, that some persons will leave the church, while others will resolve their anxiety; not only resolve it, but make something creative out of it? An answer to this question comes later. It is sufficient to note that these anxiety theories represent an understanding of how we behave.

21

Tillich. This theologian's understanding of anxiety differs from that of Kierkegaard and Niebuhr. It has as its geneological foundation an ontological dimension, namely, the understanding of being. Anxiety, for Tillich, is understood as "the state in which a being is aware of its possible nonbeing," or "anxiety is the existential awareness of nonbeing."[40] There is one phrase in Tillich's definition which gives us a clue to his intentions and. therefore, his concept of anxiety: "anxiety is the awareness of." This phrase suggests that the first step in dealing with all forms of anxiety is an "awareness of." This makes Tillich's theory different from those of Freud, Kierkegaard, and Niebuhr, as it extends beyond the function of alarm or prod to include the awareness of what is being warned or prodded about.

In *Systematic Theology* (Vol. II) he writes:

If we ask what it is that drives dreaming innocence beyond itself, we must continue our analysis of the concept "finite freedom." Man is not only finite, as is every creature; he is also aware of his finitude. And this awareness is anxiety."[41]

Later he states:

At the moment when man becomes conscious of his freedom, the awareness of his dangerous situation gets hold of him. He experiences a double threat, which is rooted in his finite freedom and expressed in anxiety. Man experiences the anxiety of losing himself by not actualizing himself and his potentialities.[42]

I find in these words what I call the anxiety dilemma. If a person does not act on his or her possible actualization and remains in the stated "dreaming innocence," then one suffers from loss of what one may become. On the other hand, if the "innocence" is given up in order to risk actualization, then one fears the loss of innocence and the possibility that the actualization may never occur.

Actualization requires a person to look at his or her finitude. Tillich points out that if a man or woman is left to his or her own "having to die," the essential anxiety about nonbeing is transformed into the horror of death. "Anxiety about nonbeing is present in everything finite. It is consciously or unconsciously effective in the whole process of living. Like the beating of the heart, it is alway present, although one is not always aware of it."[43]

Peculiar to Tillich's view of anxiety is its pointing backward to the basic anxiety-provoking event, namely, the threat to our being and potential nonbeing. It is the "awareness of" that sets off anxiety and causes persons to recognize their human condition. Persons are not in touch with this feeling at all times, but come in touch with the "awareness" frequently enough to make them anxious. All persons, sooner or later, come to the awareness of their own death and to the potential of death (not physical) within their lives.

In the research data that follows (Chapter 3) I infer that when a person gives up an important institution or friends, such as leaving the church after being active, the unrealized potential initially present in the "innocent" stage of membership triggers a type of anxiety similar to what Tillich describes.[44]

Studies on Anger

The literature on anxiety assumes anxiety as the genetic beginning of human encounter with life. It is what Schmale calls the "first psychic awareness of discomfort." From that prime experience a variety of affects follow: fear, aggression, frustration, biological withdrawal, sleep, etc. Also important, from the standpoint of this study, is the affect of anger. As anxiety is a universal affect for humans, so anger is equally ubiquitous. Anger is an emotional fact observable in every individual.[45]

For the parishioner moving away from active participation in the church, anger is a prominent experience. Characteristics of anger appear in the next chapter.

Leo Madow has collected, over the years, a list of expressions which imply an underlying anger.[46]   They fall into three categories. "The first group is modified expressions of anger . . . the second indirect expressions of anger, and the third variations of depression."[47] Madow purports that anger is disguised in many ways, some easy to recognize, some not. It may appear in language, actions, body reactions, and entertainment. Some outlets may be healthy, as in humor and vicarious participation in sports, while others bring us aches and pains. Other responses may injure us or others, or cause us to become withdrawn and depressed.[48]

At this point we need to ask several basic questions: From what does anger spring? What are its precipitants? If, as Madow points out, there are a large variety of anger effects, what is the genetic view of their beginnings?

Sullivan addresses these questions when he writes:

The other person made you angry, he humiliated you and you were annoyed, you humiliated him—all that sort of thing. But you are then missing completely the thing I am striving to describe—namely, the anxieties that started the fireworks. Until you are able to discover that the first experience in this sequence of events is acute discomfort, you won't make much sense of what I am talking about.[49]

So, according to Sullivan, we are back to anxiety as the "first psychic awareness of discomfort."

In looking at the third and fourth months of a child's life, we find somatomotor organization. When the child is able to bring objects to his or her mouth, there is a perception of pleasure and gratification. When this act is not achieved, then there is a sense of displeasure and dissatisfaction. It may also be added that "at this time there is probably only one representation developing in the mental apparatus, and this is one of undifferentiated object-world-self gratification."[50]

When gratification is not produced as expected, the child may feel what later will be more clearly perceived as anger. The feeling of anger leads the child to an intensified search to re-establish specific gratification previously experienced. Thus "anger reflects an intra-psychic awareness of fantasied object-activity. The affect of anger may reappear whenever an object-directed activity does not produce the expected results."[51] In other words, it indicates a desire to force an object to provide what is wanted.

The implications of this for the adult in the church are far reaching. When the adult reaches out for help (gratification) in the church and does not get it, the individual begins to feel the anxiety (discomfort) which leads to the affect of anger. An extensive discussion of this occurs in Chapter 4.

In Chapter 1, it was mentioned that the feelings of anger are always "object-directed." If anger functions properly and anxious feelings dissipated, the individual returns to a sense of wellbeing. Although neither anxiety nor anger are comfortable states, it is more comfortable to feel angry than anxious. When angry, we frequently find our behavior makes things worse because it tends to drive persons or things away. By driving the object away anxiety is avoided, the initial awareness of its presence fades, and the individual is left with no clear idea of how this anger came about. "In somewhere around 94% of all occasions on which you are anxious, the security operations called out by the anxiety are the things you are perfectly clear on, whereas the precipitation anxiety is obscured."[52]

Frequently, anger comes out in verbal form. "Language is one way of expressing and beginning to relieve angry feelings. The English-speaking world is fortunate; as a language, English is particularly rich because accent, intonation, and word forms carry implications not only about the role and status of the user but they also convey shades of anger . . ."[53] Language, as an expresser of anger, also reinforces group cohesiveness. It is unfortunate that the expression of anger in the church has not always been productive. My research indicates that apathetic and bored church members do not use their anger creatively.

In some sub-cultures the language of anger is a natural part of the environment. John R. Coleman in *Blue-Collar Journal: A College President's Sabbatical* talks about the naturalness of angry language among the blue collar workers who dug in the ditches next to him:

Goddamnit, Stanley, do you see what the fuck you've done: You've gone and got us all upset. You're a menace just bein' around.[54]

Such statements are typical of the language in that sub-culture and are as freely expressed as one would repeat the Lord's Prayer in a worship service.

The important issue about anger is that its expressions are various. Both verbal and nonverbal clues are important to note. These are the first indications that an individual is "off-balance," and represents the sorting process which accompanies anger.[55]

The use and control of anger is of major importance to the individual within the church. Anger is not pathological, but rather a natural process. The healthy person gets angry. Each of the developmental crises that a child, youth, and adult goes through has its anxiety/anger provoking circumstances. The healthy person works each of these through as it comes so that the next set of events may be met and integrated.[56]

Associated with anger is frustration. Anastasia and associates[57] studied anger responses of college students. They found that 52% of the anger responses were due to thwarted plans, and 20.9% consisted of situations of inferiority and loss of prestige.

Other occasions in which anger is likely to occur are under the stress of noise (human or mechanical). Saltzman[58] defines noise as discordant sound having no definite pitch. Anger can also be generated under certain conditions of touch. The phrase, "don't touch me," brings feelings of distance and anger. Another stimulus which tends to trigger anger is the sudden perception of light, e.g., being awaken from sleep, meditation or concentration. It has been reported by Peterson[59] that during heat waves the tendency to become angry increases with the rise of the temperature. When people are hungry and/or tired, they also tend to become angry.[60]

Other studies of anger have included stresses which occur from body dysfunction, mental duress, the pull of expectation not achieved, and the push of aversive action.[61]

The way in which people deal with anger varies considerably. I have found, both in literature and my research, evidence that persons tend to follow two major behavioral tracks once anger has been triggered (see Anxiety/Anger Complex on page 4). The extreme expression of anger is murder. At this level there are no controls. The super-ego is deficient and does not provide a check for deterring the overwhelming feelings.

Anger may appear in the form of projection. In its extreme form it is seen as paranoia, where the individual says: "You do not like me; no one likes me; why are you against me and trying to do me in?" The logic of the paranoid personality goes as follows: "I do not like you; you do not like me; therefore, you are against me." Paranoid personalities utilize

25

projection as a major defense against recognition of unacceptable impulses and motives. The result of this projection is that persons will frequently feel belittled, misjudged, and bear grudges because they feel thwarted by others whom they believe are against them.[62]

Anger may be so threatening that it is either repressed (involuntary) or suppressed (voluntary).[63] If anger is not conscious, the tendency is to act on that feeling rather than feeling it directly. This is commonly called "acting-out." The result of "acting-out" is frequently destructive to one's self as well as to others.

In an abortion study completed by my wife, Dr. Mary Anna Friederich, a majority of the women who came for abortions had become pregnant in relation to some form of loss or the establishment of a new relationship. The loss inevitably caused not only grief, but also anger. In one case in which we both were involved, an "acting-out" situation was observed.

A young 23-year old, white, unmarried woman called asking to see me because she was pregnant and was considering an abortion. I set a date with her, and we discussed the problem. In that interview, I discovered she had broken up with a boy friend whom she had dated for seven years. She claimed she was not angry at him, but had initiated the break because he could not make up his mind to marry her. It was obvious to me that her volunteering the information was a way of defending against some strong anger about him. The interview resulted in her decision to have the abortion. She was also interviewed by my wife. Our collaboration agreed there was an immense amount of anger being expressed in non-creative ways: two weeks after breaking up with her boy friend, she started to date another young man. On the second date they had sexual relations, and she became pregnant.

At my urging, the young woman returned for eight additional sessions to see if she could work through some of those feelings which at first were not evident to her. On about the fifth session, she got in touch with that anger. It expressed itself in crying, swearing, aggressive body actions, sweating, and verbal phrases which expressed deep loss and frustration along with a fear that no one else might like her. By the end of the eighth session, she was able to come to grips with most of her anger and seemed to be able to stay in touch with it.

Other common forms of "acting-out" in our society are drugs (including excessive drinking of alcoholic beverages) and running away (usually seen in the teenage culture, but also noted in adults who leave their families without notice).

The other track which a person can take is to turn the anger in on the self. Since the feelings are toward the self, this is called "person-blame-bias." Just as anger in its extreme form can turn one to murder, so anger for the inward-directed person can turn to suicide. This is a result of extreme depression. Aspects of guilt and shame are associated with inward-directed persons; rather than taking their anger out on the world outside of the self, they turn it back upon themselves in order not to feel the guilt and shame which would occur if the outside world reacted to their anger. This is commonly known as displacement. Displacement is the function of repressed anger which, instead of acting-out, the person "acts-in." The result of "acting-in" is frequently seen as a conversion system in which physical symptoms, i.e., migraine headaches, peptic ulcers, and other psychosomatic disorders occur.[65]

Displacement has an interesting biblical analogue. There is a process called miasma, which occurred in the Cannanite culture, prior to the entrance of the Hebrews into that land, and became a theological issue in the New Testament. Miasma still operates today.

The miasmic ritual occurred in the spring of the year. The temple priests summoned all the people together and, through a form of ritual exorcism, took the guilt and sins from the people and exorcised it into an animal (similar to Jesus placing the demon into the herd of swine). After the exorcism was completed, the animal was sent into the desert for a period of ten days where the "evil spirits left the animal." After the ten day period the animal was returned to the community. The animal was usually a goat, and to this day we call that process "scape-goating." Scape-goating is the act of blaming someone else for what you are feeling. It is a form of displacement—placing the guilt on the other—even though it is yourself who is feeling guilty. It is, in fact, the opposite of projection.

When a person finds no way out, even after being angry, the person begins to feel the affect of hopelessness. The hopeless feeling has as its counterpart helplessness, which stems from the first track mentioned above. Depending which track the person has taken, the affect of helplessness or hopelessness will become a possibility in that person's life. It is important to look at the inferences to the helpless and hopeless person and then ultimately the final stage of the movement to apathy and boredom.

Studies on Helplessness and Hopelessness

Two affects persons leaving the church exhibit are helplessness and hopelessness. A description of these affects and their genetic base follows.

The helpless and hopeless phenomenon is perceived by Schmale and Engel as "The Giving Up—Given Up Complex."[66] In other words, it is the process of letting go, of giving up and reserving energy for what is to come.

This complex involves unpleasant, distressing feelings expressed in such terms as, "It's too much," "It's no use, I can't take it any more,"

"I give up," and the like. These affects are sometimes seen by the person as failures or deficiencies in his or her environment (helplessness), and sometimes as his or her own personal failures or inadequacies for which he or she feels nothing can be done (hopelessness).

The individual experiencing these affects also perceives himself or herself as less intact, less competent, less in control, less gratified, and less capable of functioning in one's accustomed behaviors, though one may continue to attempt to do so. Relationships or roles are felt as insecure or ungratifying. The person may claim to be suffering or threatened with a disruption of a relationship, role, or goal, or one may experience rejection by persons of importance.

The person going through this stage states that the external environment, based on past experience, no longer serves as a useful guide for current or future behavior.

The giving-up person feels a loss of continuity and sequence between past and future. The person feels unable to project into the future with hope or confidence. Therefore, the future may appear relatively bleak or unrewarding.

As a result, the person is prone to revive memories (give us the good 'ol days when Pastor Jones was here). In contrast to the good feelings that might be revived, there may be feelings attributed to the past which bring up the unsuccessful or frustrating aspects of one's life.

Schmale and associates [67] describe the physical dimensions of the helplessness-hopelessness affects. Forty college students volunteered to be hypnotized and reproduce through the hypnotic state what it would feel like to be helpless and hopeless (other affects were also explored in the project). The following verbatum accounts are taken from their report:

Helplessness—The subjects were observed to look down, shrug their shoulders with an extending and turning of the forearms and palms off into space. Drawings depicted an isolated or boxed in small self usually brown. Ideation included themes of inability to move or act because of the absence of an environmental object; also thoughts of being abandoned or ideas of going crazy. The dimensions of unpleasant, inactive and time present are representative of helplessness.

Hopelessness—Posture revealed a loss of muscle tone with the body and extremeties slumping to the floor, face down. If there was anything in the environment to physically lean on, this was used to support their weight. Sensations of cold, empty, old, and limp were reported. Drawings revealed a predominance of black horizontal lines with an occasional representation of an object below the line. Thoughts revealed themes of death, futility, no future, everything bleak and desolate, nothing mattered. Thus hopelessness is an unpleasant, inactive avoidance of the self in time present. [68]

In the above illustration and in those that follow, it will be noted that these materials come primarily from a medical setting. What I have found to be important is that the feelings (affect) of an individual leaving the church community are similar. Because of the similarity, I believe it is theoretically fruitful to draw upon the medical-psychological model of helplessness and hopelessness. Schmale's work, "Giving Up as a Final Common Pathway to Changes in Health,"[69] bears directly upon individuals in the life of the church.

In a study of 190 medically ill and hospitalized individuals and 50 psychologically ill and hospitalized individuals, Schmale found that four out of five patients studied showed evidence of a recent (pre-symptom or sign of disease) experience of an actual, threatened, or symbolic loss of a highly valued form of gratification with feelings of either helplessness or hopelessness.

The information for this study was gathered through an open-ended interview. This is also true of my research, and thus, a common problem is found in both studies. Schmale remarks that, "It is only through the relationship between the investigator and the subject which exists during the time of the interview that it is possible to obtain the very personal reactions of the patient to various life events."[70]

From these interviews the investigators were able to sort out differences between the helpless and hopeless affects.

These two feelings represent two distinct and separate ways in which individuals feel themselves unable to come or find a solution to a perceived loss of desired gratification and thus, experience giving-up. The giving-up process was found as an antecedent to disease of all categories, from infectious and metabolic to those of degenerative and neoplastic origin in the medical group and from acute organic brain syndromes and schizophrenic reaction to psychoneurotic disorders and the clinical syndromes of depression in the psychiatric group.[71]

Helplessness is defined as:

. . . a feeling of being deprived, let down or left out which was preceived as coming from a change in a relationship about which the individual felt powerless to do anything. The gratification which was lost was something the individual felt he could not go on without. Thus, he had to wait for its return, which for him usually meant the return of a highly valued object in the external world to provide the gratification desired.

Hopelessness is defined as:

. . . a feeling of frustration, despair or futility perceived as coming from a loss of satisfaction for which the individual himself assumed complete and final responsibility and nothing more could be done that would undo the failure.[72]

It is recognized in Schmale's study that these affects have very early beginnings in the human's life. The affect of helplessness is first experienced during the sensitive period of separation. Freud calls this separation, "separation anxiety;" Benedek calls it "beginning confidence," while Erikson relates this stage to "initial trust." The developmental stage is that period from nine to sixteen months of age when the infant recognizes his or her dependence on an external mothering object for one's gratification. If the child can tolerate the absences of mother during this period, even if at times by the means of denial, he or she will begin to master the feelings of helplessness through an active exploration and engagement with other external objects.

Hopelessness, on the other hand, comes as an affect first experienced between the ages of three and six years. This stage involves the sensitive period of infantile sexual role differentiation. One soon discovers that regardless of how hard one tries, one cannot succeed in being the preferred object over the parent. That is, the child cannot have the chosen parent for his or her own "mate." The capacity to tolerate this perception is "aided by the psychic defense of repression which allows the child to enter latency where he has a great spurt in intellectual development without the continued awareness of feeling inadequate (Erikson's periods of initiative and industry)." [73]

From these roots in early childhood a person is conditioned to one's behavior. When the adult feels the affects of either helplessness or hopelessness, clues are drawn from previous experiences of coping effectively or ineffectively.

In Schmale's "Giving Up—Given Up Complex," it was found that the complex does not cause disease, but disease frequently (80%) appears in experiencing the complex. The giving-up part of the complex indicates the inability of the individual "to let go or give up wished-for gratification which has been lost (helplessness) or to give up self-selected goals or ambitions which are unattainable (hopelessness). The giving up part of the complex indicates the resolution phase of the complex . . ." [74] Similar aspects are found in the parishioner who leaves an active role in the church.

The profound issue of giving-up is that it occurs repeatedly throughout life as a part of growth. There are many milestones which require a change in a person's expectations of others and goals for one's self. These include: graduation, leaving home, college, military service, career, marriage, pregnancy and birth of children, buying a home, menopause, retirement, loss of parents and siblings, change of geographical location, loss of friends, etc. Even though these events can be planned for and their distress lessened, they still require the person to face loss of gratifications or goals which have to be given up intrapsychically.

This intense loss comes in the form of grief. The way an individual deals with this grieving largely determines the final resolution of the problem. Grieving passes through a number of stages as the person resolves the loss of an important object. There is the initial denial. This is followed by a gradual recall of memories of the gratifications as well as the displeasures provided by the object (this could also be an institution, i.e., the church). The feeling of helplessness occurs next. This requires a period of empathy and support before the individual can begin to go on to the next phase. The next step is to work through the memories of satisfaction and failure which resulted from the individual's activities thought to have provided pleasure or displeasure. The final stage is the feeling of hopelessness. There is nothing that the grieving individual can do to change the fate of the lost object. It is only after this last stage has been completed (the acceptance of the loss of the object), that new roles are assumed for relating. The future can then be faced with hope.

Grief is experienced by the person who has strong attachments to the church and then leaves. This aspect will be developed in Chapter 4.

Studies on Apathy and Boredom

Following the stages of helplessness and hopelessness come the affects of apathy and boredom. As helplessness and hopelessness are the stages of the person giving-up, apathy and boredom represent those final stages of having given up. To place these four affects in their proper sequence, we must note that helplessness is followed by apathy, while hopelessness is followed by boredom. Apathy and boredom are not qualitatively different, rather they represent an intrapsychic direction, either toward the outside world of others (apathy) or the inner world of self (boredom).

Both positions emerge when the individual's energy source is depleted. When depletion is felt, residual strength is maintained through a holding pattern. This is seen in Engel's and Schmale's "conservation-withdrawal," which is biologically directed, but is also noted in the psychic process as well.[75] "We can deduce, but cannot document, the core subjective experience of conservation-withdrawal to include feelings of decreased strength, energy and interest in the outside world . . ."[76]

Viktor Frankl also speaks of the problem of boredom in the logotherapeutic terms of the "loss of meaning." He calls boredom an "existential vacuum," and points out that 55% of the staff of the hospital in which he worked exhibited some degree of boredom:

In actual fact, boredom is now causing, and certainly bringing to psychiatrists, more problems to solve than is distress. And these problems are growing increasingly crucial, for progressive automation will probably lead to an enormous increase in leisure hours of average workers. The pity of it is that many of them will not know what to do with all their newly acquired free time.[78]

Frankl's "loss of meaning" speaks strongly of the church members who no longer see the church as providing important input for their lives. There is a parallel to the helpless-hopeless phenomenon when giving-up is taking place. When meaninglessness occurs, there is a tendency to give up the relationships with persons who were once important.

Brewer and associates report in a research project dealing with meaningful church relationships that the essence of the church is not the view that the minister holds but the one that is communicated by the lay people:

As this parish study indicates, the average layman's faith and his understanding of the church are not so much the product of the sermons he hears but what he absorbs from other laymen around him. Not the preacher but other laymen are the prime communicators. [79]

Along with meaninglessness which accompanies apathy and boredom, many turn away from the church with a feeling of indifference. This is expressed in terms of, "I don't care anymore," or "Who cares about what happens to the church!"

Frequently, persons in the church have interpreted this indifference (apathy and boredom) as a kind of sin, a rejecting of the church and ultimately the Kingdom of God. In more secular terms Menninger puts it as follows:

Their real opposition—the common enemy, if you please—is something else. It is the evil, the destructiveness in the world, and more especially, it is the complacency of the comfortable. It is the indifference, the apathy, the hardness of heart which troubles neither to believe nor to doubt, but simply does not care. The common enemy is not some starry-eyed idealist, nor even, as Norman Cousins says, "some powerful nation or totalitarian power controlling world ideology." It is rather the man whose only concern about the world is that it stay in one piece during his lifetime." [80]

It is this "piece" that the apathetic and bored person tries to preserve. They feel they must withdraw from the anxiety-provoking situation or lose control, go crazy, or be so overwhelmed that they will not be able to function and will lose everything. Rather than lose their total being, they move far enough away to preserve part of the self. In preserving that part, they have to sacrifice a meaningful aspect of their lives. This is the dilemma of the apathetic or bored church member.

NOTES

[1] Research figures were taken from the Annual Conference Year Books of the Western New York Conference of the United Methodist Church for the years of 1965-1974 and compiled by the conference statistician for presentation at the meeting held at Houghton College, June 11-14, 1974.

[2] George Gallup Poll as quoted in *The Cleveland Press*, April, 1967.

[3] George Gallup Poll, quoted in *Information Service*, Vol. XLVI, No. 2, January 28, 1967.

[4] Constant H. Jacquet, Jr., Editor, *Yearbook of American and Canadian Churches 1974* (Nashville: Abingdon Press, 1974), p. 262

[5] Gallup, *Information Service*, 1967.

[6] Jacquet, Jr., Editor, *Yearbook 1974*, p. 262.

[7] Jacquet, Jr., Editor, *Yearbook 1974*, p. 262.

[8] Douglas W. Johnson and George W. Cornell, *Punctured Preconceptions* (New York: Friendship Press, 1972), p. 37.

[9] Michael Argyle, *Religious Behaviour* (London: Rootledge and Kegan Paul, 1958), p. 31.

[10] Thomas C. Campbell and Yoshio Fukuyama, *The Fragmented Layman* (Philadelphia: Pilgrim Press, 1970), p. 77.

[11] Sidney L. Pressey and Raymond G. Kuhlen, *Psychological Development Through the Life Span* (New York: Harper & Brothers, 1957), p. 486.

[12] J. H. Fichter, The Profile of Catholic Religious Life," *American Journal of Sociology* (1952) 58:145-150.

[13] Douglas W. Johnson, Paul R. Picard, Bernard Quinn, *Churches and Church Membership in the United States* (Washington, D.C.: Glenmary Research Center, 1971), pp. X-XI.

[14] Harry Stack Sullivan, *The Psychiatric Interview* (New York: W. W. Norton & Company, Inc., 1970), p. 100.

[15] Sullivan, *Psychiatric Interview*, p. 100.

[16] David S. Dustin, *How Psychologists Do Research: The Example of Anxiety* (Englewood Cliffs, N.J.: Prentice-Hall, Inc., 1969), p. 3.

[17] Dustin, *How Psychologists Do Research*, pp. 22-27.

[18] Dustin, *How Psychologists Do Research*, pp. 66-73.

[19] M. H. Lader (ed.), "Studies of Anxiety," *British Journal of Psychiatry Special Publication No. 3* (Asford, Kent: Headley Brothers, Ltd., 1967).

[20] Murray Parkes, "Separation Anxiety: An Aspect of the Search for a Lost Object," *British Journal of Psychiatry Special Publication No. 3*, ed. M. H. Lader (Asford, Kent: Headley Brothers Ltd., 1967), pp. 87-92.

[21] John Bowlby, "Processes of Mourning," *International Journal of Psychoanalysis* (1961), Vol. 62, p. 317.

[22] W. B. Douglas and M. Bloomfield, *Children Under Five* (Fair Lawn, N.J.: Essential Books, 1958).

[23] Arthur H. Schmale, Jr., "A Genetic View of Affects," *The Psychoanalytical Study of the Child* (1964), XIX, p. 289.

[24] William F. Fischer, *Theories of Anxiety* (New York: Harper & Row, 1970), p. 119.

[25] Several outstanding men in the physiological field of anxiety are A. F. Ax, G. Bergmann, K. W. Spence, P. R. Breggin, A. Buss, W. B. Cannon, and S. Schachtel.

[26] M. Heidegger, *Being and Time* (New York: Harper & Row, 1963), pp. 1-438.

33

[27] Works which back up these concepts are: K. Goldstein, "On Emotions," *Journal of Psychology*, XIX (1951), pp. 37-46; *The Organism: A Holistic Approach to Biology Derived from Pathological Data in Man* (Boston: Beacon Press, 1963).

[28] Karl Menninger, *The Vital Balance* (New York: The Viking Press, 1963), pp. 127-134.

[29] John Cowper Powys, *The Meaning of Culture* (New York: Norton, 1929), p. 274.

[30] Seward Hiltner and Karl Menninger (eds.), *Constructive Aspects of Anxiety* (New York: Abingdon Press, 1963), p. 26.

[31] Robert Bretall (ed.), *A Kierkegaard Anthology* (Princeton: Princeton University Press, 1947).

[32] Walter Lowrie (trans.), *The Concept of Dread* by Soren Kierkegaard (Princeton: Princeton University Press, 1944). Walter Lowrie's translation of "dread" should have been "anxiety."

[33] Lowrie (trans.), *Dread*, p. 14.

[34] Lowrie (trans.), *Dread*, p. 27.

[35] Lowrie (trans.), *Dread*, p. 38.

[36] Lowrie (trans.), *Dread*, p. 55.

[37] Hiltner and Menninger (eds.), *Anxiety*, pp. 60-61.

[38] Reinhold Niebuhr, *The Nature and Destiny of Man: A Christian Interpretation* (New York: Charles Scribner & Sons, 1941), Vol. VIII.

[39] Hiltner and Menninger (eds.), *Anxiety*, pp. 60-61.

[40] Paul Tillich, *The Courage To Be* (New Haven: Yale University Press, 1956), p. 35.

[41] Paul Tillich, *Systematic Theology*, Vol. II (Chicago: University of Chicago Press, 1957), p. 534.

[42] Tillich, *Systematic Theology*, pp. 35-36.

[43] Tillich, *Systematic Theology*, p. 67.

[44] Tillich, *Courage*, p. 41.

[45] Frederic R. Sterns, *Anger: Psychology, Physiology, Pathology* (Springfield: Charles C. Thomas, 1972), p. 55.

[46] Leo Madow, *Anger* (New York: Charles Scribner's Sons, 1972).

[47] Madow, *Anger*, pp. 5-7.

[48] Madow, *Anger*, p. 13.

[49] Sullivan, *Psychiatric Interview*, p. 108.

[50] Arthur H. Schmale, Jr., "A Genetic View of Affects," *The Psychoanalytical Study of the Child*, XIX (1964), p. 290.

[51] Schmale, "Genetic View," p. 291.

[52] Sullivan, *Psychiatric Interview*, p. 108.

[53] Derek Miller, *Adolescence: Psychology, Psychopathology, and Psychotherapy* (New York: Jason Aronson, 1974), pp. 230-231.

[54] John R. Coleman, *Blue-Collar Journal: A College President's Sabbatical* (Philadelphia: J. B. Lippincott Company, 1974), p. 28.

[55] Miller, *Adolescence*, p. 233.

[56] Committee on Child Psychiatry, *Psychopathological Disorders in Childhood* (New York: Jason Aronson, 1974). p. 49.

[57] A. Anastasia, W. Cohen, and D. A. Spatz, "A Study of Fear and Anger in College Students Through the Controlled Diary Method," *Journal of General Psychology*, Vol. 73 (1948), p. 243.

[58] M. Saltzman, *Clinical Audiology* (New York: Grune & Stratton, 1949).

[59] W. F. Peterson, *Man—Weather—Sun* (Springfield: Charles C. Thomas, 1948).

[60] P. T. Young, "Laughing and Weeping, Cheerfulness and Depression. A Study of Moods Among College Students," *Journal of Social Psychology*, Vol. 8 (1937), p. 311.

[61] Sterns, *Anger*, pp. 3-12.

62 Theodore Lidz, *The Person* (New York: Basic Books, Inc., 1968), p. 515.

63 Lidz, *Person*, p. 257.

64 Mary Anna Friederich, "Abortion: A Three Year Follow-Through," (unpublished: information was given through lectures at several medical conventions which I attended).

65 Lidz, *Person*, p. 515.

66 Arthur H. Schmale, Jr., George L. Engel, "The Giving Up—Given Up Complex," *Arch. Gen. Psychiatry*, Vol. 17 (August, 1967), pp. 135-136; see also George L. Engel, "A Life Setting Conducive to Illness," *Annals of Internal Medicine*, Vol. 69 (August, 1968), No. 2.

67 A. Schmale, D. Tinling, L. Eby, "Experimental Induction of Affects," *ACTA Medica Psychosomatica* (proceedings of the 7th European Conference on Psychosomatic Research, Rome, September 11-16, 1967).

68 A. Schmale and Associates, "Experimental Induction," pp. 6-7.

69 A. H. Schmale, "Giving Up as a Final Common Pathway to Changes in Health," *Adv. Psychosomatic Medicine*, Vol. 8, pp. 20-40.

70 Schmale, "Final Common Pathway," pp. 22-23.

71 Schmale, "Final Common Pathway," p. 23.

72 Schmale, "Final Common Pathway," p. 23.

73 Schmale, "Final Common Pathway," p. 24.

74 Schmale, "Final Common Pathway," p. 25.

75 George L. Engel and Arthur H. Schmale, "Conservation-Withdrawal: A Primary Regulatory Process for Organismic Homeostasis," *Physiology Emotion and Psychosomatic Illness*, 1972, pp. 57-73.

76 Engel, Schmale, "Conservation-Withdrawal," p. 72.

77 For an extended list of research on helplessness, hopelessness, apathy and boredom by Engel, Schmale and a host of others, see "Conservation-Withdrawal," pages 73-75 where over 65 research projects are listed.

78 Viktor E. Frankl, *Man's Search for Meaning* (New York: Washington Square Press, Inc., 1964), pp. 168-169.

79 Earl D. D. Brewer and Associates, *Protestant Parish* (Atlanta: Communicative Arts Press, 1967), p. 20.

80 Menninger, *The Vital Balance*, p. 375.

Chapter 3

Analysis of Data

INTRODUCTION

This chapter is devoted to a systematic examination of the research data gathered through interviews with 101 persons. The research was conducted in four suburban United Methodist Churches, located in the Western New York Conference of the United Methodist Church. The churches were Christ View United Methodist Church, Henrietta; Orchard Park United Methodist Church, Orchard Park; Fairport United Methodist Church, Fairport; and Epworth United Methodist Church, Jamestown.

A review of the research procedures in Chapter 1 will help recall the process used in gathering the data through an open-ended interview. Interviews were held in the homes for 97 persons, with four others secured over the telephone. The four phone interviews did not show any unusual or different characteristics than the home inquiries, except there was not as much detailed information secured. In spite of this, the four were added into the general tabulation and have become a part of the 101 persons.

METHODS IN SECURING THE SAMPLE

This sample was secured by contacting the pastors of the afore-mentioned churches, who agreed to provide me with a minimum of 15 family units in each of three categories: Group A, active members; Group B, members who were less active than a year ago; and Group C, those who were not involved in the church in any way. The reader may wish to review a more thorough description of the criteria of the A, B, and C groups in Chapter 1, pages 2-3.

Upon receiving the names and addresses of the possible partici-pants, an automatically typed letter was sent by first class mail to each family unit. (A copy of the letter can be seen in the appendix.) A return card was enclosed so the recipients could indicate their desire to decline or take part in the project. There was a basic hypothesis made at the time of the mailing that there would be a declining rate of return, with the As having the largest, the Cs the smallest, and the Bs somewhere in between.

The results of that mailing are as follows: a total of 236 letters were sent to the four churches; Christ View — 79, Fairport — 51, Orchard Park — 59, and Jamestown — 47. Of the 236 invitations, there was a return of 66 in all categories or a 28% response. There was a great diversity of return rates according to the individual churches. Christ View (the church of which I am pastor) had 45.6%, Fairport 35.3%, Orchard Park 11.8%, and Epworth 10.6%. The two churches, Orchard Park and Epworth, are of considerable distance from Christ View (75 and 150 miles respectively), while Fairport is only eight miles away. A number of the people at Fairport are acquainted with my church, and a few of them know me personally. This may account for some of the differences in the return rates.

The return rates, representing family units and broken down according to activity level (A, B, C), can be seen in Table 1 in the appendix.

According to Table 1, the A group had a higher return rate (47.4%) than did the B and C groups. There was, however, only a slight difference between the B (15.3%) and C (12.5%) groups. Though the B response was only 2% higher than the C, it fell between the A and C responses. Therefore the hypothesis stated above was supported.

I immediately recognized that the response in the B and C groups was too small for statistical purposes and more interviews were needed in those areas. There was an attempt to contact all of the B and C groups by phone (those who had been sent cards but did not return them). As a result of the phone calls, I was able to secure two more family units in the B group and ten in the C category who agreed to be interviewed. The ratio of calls and corresponding affirmative answers to a home interview was eight to one, or 12%, while the response by mail for both the B and C categories was 12.1%.

Since not all of the family units returning cards were interviewed, the total family units completing an interview will be different than Table 1. Before I come to the actual number of individuals (and family units) interviewed, it is important to note the response in securing the callers.

THE RESPONSE IN SECURING THE CALLERS

In order for the data to be gathered for this research project, it was necessary to select and train persons who would visit and interview the parishioners of the four congregations. A mimeographed letter was sent to fifty clergypersons who I personally selected. All were from the Western New York Conference of the United Methodist Church. Twenty of the fifty responded positively, stating they would come to a one day training event before making their calls. Eighteen of those who returned cards arrived for training. Two came who had not returned cards, making a total of twenty.

After the day of training, two of the trainees claimed the work was too time consuming and did not agree to call. I was left with 18 persons to make 66 calls, which was the number of cards returned (see Table 1). Before all the calls could be made, one of the pastors was moved out of the Conference, while another became ill and had major surgery. Both of these men returned their cards, and they were redistributed. Three other callers did not make their calls, even after being contacted twice. From the original 66 cards returned, 46 family units were interviewed by 13 pastors with a completion rate of 70%. From the 46 families, 83 individuals were interviewed. Adding to these figures the interviews obtained from persons who opened their homes after a phone call, a total of 60 family units with 101 individuals interviewed was achieved. The distribution of the calls can be seen in Table 2.

An analysis of the interview figures of Table 2 will show a predominance of Christ View interviews (60.4%), while Fairport (25.7%), Orchard Park (9.9%), and Epworth (3.0%) had fewer responses.

A COMPARATIVE ANALYSIS OF THE ACTIVE, LESS ACTIVE AND INACTIVE GROUPINGS

I now turn to a review of the responses, comparing each of the A, B, and C categories with the 101 interviews. Each section of the data gathering sheet (see appendix) will be explored. These sections are sociological, behavioral, precipitate, situational, religious status, and sequential religious events.

Sociological Data

The sociological data includes age distribution, financial status, occupational variations, educational levels, marital status, family size, and sex distribution.

In the following data, the differentiation between churches will be dropped, except where it is deemed necessary for interpretive purposes. The major emphasis is not on comparing one church against another but comparing active (A) members with those who have become less active (B) and those who are now completely inactive (C). It should be noted that the Cs were once As, then became Bs, and finally moved to the C grouping.

Age. The age distribution for the total sample had a predominance of persons falling in the 30 to 49 age range. Table 3 shows the distribution.

In the total sample the 20-29 age group had 8%, while on the other end of the range, 60-up, there was 5%. The 30-39 age group was the largest with 37%, while the 40-49 group had slightly less with 35%. The 50-59 age division was only slightly more than the youngest and oldest groups with 15%.

When comparing the A, B, and C groups with each of the age ranges, the 20-29 range shows that the As had 8%, Bs 0%, and Cs 13%. The 30-39 range found the As with 43%, the Bs 11%, and the Cs 39%. The next age grouping (40-49) exhibited the following: As 34%, Bs 52%, and Cs 22%. The next to oldest age range (50-59) had fewer responses than the previous two categories, with the As having 11%, the Bs 18%, and no responses for the Cs. The 60-up range was thinly represented with only 3% for the As, 18% for the Bs, and like the 50-59 range, no response for the Cs.

The largest age group in the As was the 30-39 year spread with 43%. This was comparable with Cs, who had 39% in that same age group. The Bs had a majority of their interviewees in the 40-49 age range with 52%. There is a statistically significant difference between the As and Bs (.025),[1] but there is no significant difference between the A and C categories. The Bs had a significantly older age group than did the As.

The Cs did not have any persons in the age groups beyond 40-49. Thus, no C participants from 50-up were willing to discuss their feelings about the church with the interviewers.

With the indication of the age distribution, I found a similar relationship in the financial distribution.

Family income. The income levels of this group of persons was reflective of the age distribution above, and the suburban churches from which they came. The modal average was in the $15,000 to $20,000 range, while the median average was $17,465.59. I believe that Table 4 will show an even distribution between the A, B, and C groups. Two of the churches in this study (Christ View and Fairport) are located in Monroe County. The median family income for Monroe County in 1974 was $17,765.[2] This matches the median average in my study.

There are several characteristics which need to be clarified in the C category. There is no one in the C group with an income under $10,000. The other two groups (A, B) have 14% and 18% respectively for those earning under $10,000.

The median income (50th percentile) for the C group is $15,869.26, while the As follow with the next highest amount of $17,638.72 and the Bs with the highest figure of $18,888.78. All three of the categories fall within the $15,000 - $19,999 grouping. Since the median average for the entire sample is $17,465.59, this brings the Cs under the average (-$1,596.33), while the As and Bs were above average with figures of $177.13 and $1,423.19 respectively. None of the figures show great variation and certainly fall within the suburban middle class range of income. The relationship of the As to the Bs and Cs is not statistically significant.

Occupation. The occupational spread for this sample centers around the implications of both age group and income characteristics. Using the ten classifications of the U.S. Bureau of the Census, the distribution of occupations among the employed persons of the sample has a high percentage of professional, technical and related workers (58.9%). There is a predominance of As (63.8%) in the professional group, with the Bs having 41.7% and the Cs 57.1%. The As have 22.7% more than the Bs, but that is not statistically significant. The professional category included teachers, nurses, engineers, doctors, school administrators, etc.

The other occupational groupings noted in this survey were clerical and related workers — 13.7%, sales workers — 9.6%, craftsmen/foremen and related workers — 8.2%, proprietors, managers and officials — 4.1%, and 2.7% for laborers, operatives and related workers. Other details and relationships can be seen in Table 5.

The strong bias of the group toward professional workers, with no persons in the farm or private household groups, indicates the expected type of persons that would make up the suburban church.

Educational level. The educational level of these 101 persons is predominantly college educated, with only 24% of the parishioners having a 12th grade education or under (only 2% had under 12th grade education, both were 9th grade level). The modal average of education was in the 1-3 years of college group (31.7%), but those with four years of college were close behind with 25.5%, followed by post graduates with 18.3%.

There are virtually no differences between the A, B, and C groups regarding educational level. Table 6 will allow the reader to see the similarity across the activity groupings.

Along with the educational level, we also sought to find what percentage of these persons were presently involved in some kind of formal educational program. Out of 84 responses to that question, a total of 7% were involved in part-time schooling, with no one full-time. Again there was no significant difference between the activity groups (A — 8.5%, B — 6.3%, C — 4.8%).

Marital status, sex, family size. It was expected that the large majority of the sample would be married persons. The facts are that 95% of the sample were married, with the other 5% spread among the following categories: single (1%), separated (1%), widows (2%), widowers (1%). There were no significant differences between the A, B, and C categories.

The male-female distribution indicated more females (55.5%) than

40

males (45.5%), while the family size ran the range from no children to nine. The mean average of the 60 families involved was 2.6 children per family unit. Sixty-six percent of the families had two or three children, while 17% had one or no children. On the other end of the family size, 18% had families of four or more children. When these families were compared in the A, B, and C categories, there was only one major variation; this was in the family size of three children, where the As had 22%, Bs — 36%, and Cs — 57%. In all other ages the difference was less than 10% between activity groupings. None of these categories prove to be significantly different.

Church hopping. There was an attempt on the part of the interviewers to find the pattern of this group's behavior when changing churches within the same town. In reviewing the responses, it was found that only one person out of the sample had a pattern showing attendance at more than one church in the same town without changing residence. There were several persons who changed churches, but they also had moved to a different part of the same town or city. These I did not consider, for it follows that a person moving to a new suburb will tend to locate in a neighboring church; at least the data in this research support that assumption.

Institutional Behavior

This section on institutional behavior covers a number of diverse areas centering around the behavior of the parishioner regarding the institutional church and one's related Christian faith. Areas covered begin with the perception of the interviewer about the parishioner's level of anxiety during the time of the interview. In addition, there was information gathered giving their church financial habits and involvement in committee work. Along with these activities, the percentage of attendance at worship was compared with what it was a year ago. Several tangent ideas were also considered in this section. We looked at illness in the family as a deterrent to attendance and involvement as well as interfamily conflict related to the church. The ability to articulate one's Christian faith was also sought by the interviewer and any other behaviors which the interviewer may have written. I now wish to explore these areas and share the results.

Anxiety. There was a hypothesis regarding the level of anxiety that the B and C groups would have a significantly higher level of anxiety than the A group. There were seven persons who had no anxiety level recorded, thus there were 94 persons on which this sample was taken. The interviewer was asked to place a circle around one of the numbers

41

on a scale of 1-10. One indicated a very low level of anxiety, while ten was very high. In order for the groups of anxiety levels to be more meaningful, I merged the individual numbers into two groups of three and one group of four (1-3, 4-6, 7-10). Since there were no responses at the ten level, the sample really worked out to be three groups of three.

Table 7 indicates the different levels of anxiety in the A, B, and C groupings and the intensity of the anxiety.

The differences between the A, B, and C groups at the low anxiety level (1-3) were negligible with the As (77.8%), Bs (70.6%), Cs (73.9%), and the average (75.5%). Though there was a little less anxiety with the As compared with the Bs, this very small margin was insignificant. The medium anxiety level (4-6) indicated there was less anxiety in the Bs than the other groups, but the differences were very small (A — 18.5%, B — 11.8%, C — 17.4%). The high level of anxiety (7-10) showed more deviation than the other three levels. The Bs had 17.6%, 13.9% more than the As (3.7%) and 8.9% more than the Cs (8.7%). The tendency was for the Bs to be slightly more anxious at the high level of anxiety, but the As were more anxious at the medium level. The Cs fell very close to the average and did not show much deviation from the norm of the group. There was a significant difference (.01 level) between the As and the Bs, but there was no significance between the As and Cs. The significance came at the high level of anxiety. The hypothesis was only partially supported.

Financial response. Part of the criteria for picking the A, B, and C groups is that As would be persons who support the church financially and had made a pledge during the survey year (1974). It was expected, therefore, that there would be a predominance of As who had pledged. The Bs were chosen because of pledging less or not pledging at all, and the Cs did not pledge in the survey year. The reporting of this criterion is seen in Table 8 and corroborates these hypotheses.

The figures indicate that a predominance of As did pledge (96.2%). The reason for the 3.8% not pledging in the A group is due to a few persons who contributed well but did not sign pledges. The surprising figure of 23.1% of the C group pledging came because of an unusual circumstance in the Fairport Church where individuals gave only to the building fund and sent their money directly to the bank. The local church did not know that they were giving and, therefore, put them in the C category. These Fairport Cs did not contribute financially in any other way. The Bs, on the other hand, did contribute, less frequently than the As, but considerably more than the Cs.

The above figures deal with persons who either pledged or did not pledge and represent 79.2% of the sample of 101 persons or a raw figure of 80 persons. The other 20.8% of those interviewed fell into two groups: those from whom we had no response (7.9%), and those that responded that they contributed but did not pledge (12.9%). Those who contributed, but did not pledge, represent 13 persons or 12.9% of the 101 interviewed. Of those 13 persons the A, B, and C breakdown was as follows: A — 30.8%, B — 15.4%, C — 53.8%. These figures indicate that there was considerable difference in percentage between C and A-B groups. In comparison to the other groups, more persons in the C group contributed but did not pledge. There is no significant difference between the As and Bs, but there is a .001 level of significance between the As and Cs.

Service. As the finance groupings were determined ahead of time by my criteria for the different group levels, so serving the church was also predetermined and is reflected in the statistics. It would be expected that the As would have a considerably higher rate of involvement than the Cs. The response follows that pattern and can be seen in Table 9.

The figures clearly show response to church activity and are indicative of how the individuals were chosen for the sample. The As did not have a 100% activity rate because, in a few cases, the husband or wife held a committee position and their mate did not. These figures also indicate that the Bs were not inclined to be on committees (76.4%), although 23.5% did serve on at least one committee. The Cs proved to be 100% non-involved at the committee level. These figures prove that the requirements for each of the groups were met regarding their activity levels. There is a .001 level of significance between the As and Bs, as well as the As and Cs.

Worship attendance. Along with the financial and service aspect of the sample, worship attendance was also a criterion for choosing individuals according to activity levels. The statistical responses are ranked according to the expected results, with the As having the highest attendance of 77.9% attending worship 75% or more of the time. No As were in the 0-25% attendance level, while 100% of the Cs were in the lowest grouping, and no C was in the 75-up attendance level. The Bs fell largely in the 0-25% group, with 52.9% of them attending less than once a month. Only 11.7% of the Bs attended 75% or more of the time. Table 10 will show other less important relationships between the groups, as well as those I have just cited. There is a significant difference between the As and Bs and also the A and C categories at the .001 level.

Not all of the pre-selected A couples fell in the A grouping. I made one call where the husband was an A, but the wife was a C. In other words, the husband attended worship alone and also took part in the life of the church alone. Given the above possible exceptions, the results of the findings were what was expected under the circumstances provided by the selection process.

One other aspect of the attendance response which is meaningful and helpful is the change of worship practices over the past year. The yes responses to any major change in worship attendance over the past year are as follows: A — 13.6%, B — 23.5%, C — 26.0%. While there is a tendency for the Cs to have more movement away from activity, the largest movement is from active to less active (A to B), rather than from less active to inactive. In inquiring about these changes, I found that change was not always toward the negative but could also be toward more activity. In order to find that tendency, I charted the movement both upward and downward. Table 11 shows the results.

The movement represented by Table 11 shows the As were the only group having movement toward more frequency in worship. The Bs and Cs all had negative responses. In other words, no Bs or Cs interviewed had changed their worship patterns to a more frequent pattern. The As not only had a response of more frequency in worship, they also had some negative response, with persons attending less frequently (6.5%). However, when taking the increase (11.5%) over and against the losses (6.5%), the As made a gain in worship frequency of 5%. In contrast to the As, the Bs had a loss of 23.5%, while the Cs had a change downward of 26.1%. There is no significant difference in response between the As and Bs, but a significant difference exists between the As and Cs.

Illness in families. This statistic is very simple and basically insignificant. Out of the sample of 101 persons, three (2.97%) shared that the reason for the change of worship attendance and other activities in the church was due to personal or family illness. There was one person in each of the A, B, and C groups.

Ability to articulate the Christian faith. Should persons active in the church (As) be able to articulate their Christian faith better than those who are inactive? This question is answered in the response that we received from our investigation. Table 12 gives the details.

This table indicates that all persons in the A group were able to articulate their faith at a moderate or excellent level, while the Bs (47.1%) and the Cs (21.7%) were in the no articulation category. These statistics were achieved by observing the frequency in which individuals used religious language to describe their life setting and religious commitment. There is good indication that those who are moving away or have moved away verbalize their faith less than those highly involved in the church. Why that occurs will be discussed in the next chapter. Does the person who is not able to articulate his or her faith move from the church more easily than those who speak more freely of their faith in God? The big differences in the groups come not at the moderate level of articulation where there is little deviation (A — 66.1%, B — 47.1%, C — 52.2%), but in the no articulation and excellent levels. Compared with the As, the Cs tend to hold their own at the excellent level

(A — 33.9%, C — 23.1%), while the Bs fall to a low 5.8%. It appears that the Bs have more difficulty in expressing their faith than either the Cs or As. Statistically there is a .001 level of significance between the As and Bs as well as the As and Cs.

Other behaviors. There were very few comments made by the interviewers in this category. Those that were made did not yield anything of great importance. The remarks were primarily comments on how the interview went (all comments were positive) and occasionally a statement regarding the depth that a person was hurt (C group) in the changing of pastors.

This concludes the statistical work on the second category. We now turn to the precipitants of church inactivity and explore those factors involved in causing a person to change his or her relationship with the church congregation.

Precipitants

The following precipitants are discussed in the sections below: conflict with — pastor, church members, family members, moral values, theological, financial, and educational issues; overworked in the church; levels of community involvement; personal problems such as deaths in family, and divorce or separation from mate; feeling of not being needed; and being misdirected.

Conflict with pastor. The differentiation between the A, B, and C groups regarding conflict with the pastor shows an interesting pattern and some significant differences. Table 13 shows the varying responses.

The responses of the A group show a distinct variation from the Cs, with the As having 4.2%, while the Cs had 45.5% of their group responding to high conflict. The Bs had no one in the high category but did have a predominance of response in the moderate range, where the As had 18.8%, Bs — 31.3% and Cs — 9.0%. In looking at the Cs alone, the reader will note that the Cs seem to fall into one of two categories; they are either in the no conflict group (45.5%) or in the high conflict group (45.5%), with the moderate level being 9.0%. In contrast to the Cs, the As are largely (77.0%) in the no conflict group, with 18.8% in the moderate and only 4.2% in the high. The Bs, on the other hand, fall about half way between in the no conflict group with 68.8% responding. The Bs have the largest response (31.2%) of the three groups in the moderate range and no response in the high.

There is a significant difference (.001) between the As and the Cs, but there is no significance between the As and Bs. The implications of conflict with the pastor are discussed in the following chapter.

Conflict with another church member. The study of active church members in comparison to less active and non-active members shows that conflict with another church member is of major importance. Table 14 shows the difference in distribution between the groups.

The As had 74% of the respondents not reporting conflict with other church members, while the Bs and Cs had 57% and 54% respectively. The major differences were shown at the high level of conflict. Here the As had only 6%, while the Bs had 7% and the Cs 32%. In the moderate level of conflict there were no major differences (A — 21%, B — 36%, C — 14%). Statistically, there is no significance between the As and Bs, but there is a .025 level of significance between the As and the Cs. The inactive (C) member has a greater level of conflict with other church members than the less active (B) or active (A) parishioner.

Conflict with a family member. Table 15 describes the difference between the groups and shows there is a significant difference between the As, Bs, and Cs. The As had almost no conflict within their families around church issues, or at least none that were unresolvable. The As had 90% responding at the no conflict level, with the Bs showing 41% and the Cs 63%. Again it is the high level of conflict that points out the major difference, with the As having 5%, the Bs 21% and the Cs 26%. In comparison with the active church member, the less active and the non-active member have significantly more conflict around church issues than do those who are active.

Conflict with theological issues. When comparing the active members with the less active and non-active, there is no significant difference between the groups regarding theological matters. Though there are leanings toward more conflict with both B and C groups, there is not a statistically significant difference. For details of the response, the reader may turn to Table 16 in the appendix.

Conflict over financial issues. Conflict over financial matters in the church shows up as being significant between the As and the Cs (.001 level) but is not significant between the As and Bs. At the no conflict level the As and Bs had no responses, while the Cs had 20%. Only the Cs showed a major difference in behavior over money issues in the church. A rationale for these differences is given in the next chapter. For other percentages which might interest the reader, turn to Table 17.

Conflict over educational issues. There is a significant difference between the A and B groups over educational matters but no major difference between the A and C groups. At the no conflict level the As had 86%, Bs 43% and Cs 74%. It is at the high level of conflict that the major difference occurs between the A and B groups with the As having 4% and the Bs 29%. For other details see Table 18.

Overworked in church activities. All categories of church members (see Table 19) show that there are some who feel that they are overworked in the church. When making the comparison between the As, Bs, and Cs, there is a statistically significant level for both the Bs and Cs in comparison with the As (Bs — .005, C — .05). At the no conflict level, the As show 82%, the Bs 55% and the Cs 53%. At the high conflict level the As have only 2%, while the Bs have 36% and the Cs 18%. There is one unusual characteristic about this category of being overworked; the moderate level of being overworked is higher (16%) for the As than for the Bs (9%).

Involvement in other community activities. Table 20 shows the unusual characteristics of the findings regarding the involvement of this sample in other community activities. There is a relatively high proportion of these persons who are not involved in any community activity, regardless of whether they are involved in the church or not. For example, the As have 36%, Bs 62%, and Cs 50% of their populations in the no involvement category. This indicates that the Bs have the highest (62%) of the three groups. There is some indication that the Bs and Cs have a considerably higher level of involvement in the community than do the As, who are already active in the church. There is, however, an unusual twist when we observe the results of the involvement at the high level. This level indicates that the As have 9%, the Bs 38%, and the Cs 18%. The category of community activities is one of the few statistics in this study which shows that the less active member in the church is more active in the community than the active church group. In this case, the Bs far outweigh the As in community involvement. Since there are no Bs in the moderate level but there are 55% of the As in that category, it is obvious that the differences between these two groups are significantly different (.005 level). There is no significant difference between the As and Cs.

Responses to the concept of seeing God as active in the world. In this open-ended interview, information was gathered on the person's concept of how they saw God as being active in the world. The interviewers were asked to indicate the responses of seeing God as non-active, moderate or high in activity. The results are seen in Table 21.

The reader will find that at the no activity level the As have only 5%, while the Bs have 26%. The Cs have approximately the same as the As with 4%. At the moderate level the As have 47%, Bs 53%, and the Cs 70%. The As find God more active (48%) at the high level than any of the other groups. The Bs had 20%, with the Cs at 26% of their populations seeing God as highly active in the world. These statistics indicate there is a highly significant difference between the As and Cs, though there is a strong leaning toward God being more active in the world for the As than for the Cs at the high level.

Sees God as outside or inside of self. The purpose of this rather different category was to find if the interviewees perceived God as being more active outside of the self or inside of self. I previously hypothesized that the As would have an integrated concept of God exhibiting both inward and outward orientations toward God. It was expected that the less active and inactive persons would have different orientations. The tabulation in Table 22 calls the hypothesis into question.

The percentages of persons seeing God outside of self according to activity categories are: As 20%, Bs 43%, and Cs 34%. These figures indicate a trend that the less active see God more frequently as outside of self than do the active members. When looking at the balanced concept of seeing God both inwardly and outwardly, the results are as follows: As 53%, Bs 36%, and Cs 48%. Here my hypothesis was affirmed that the active member would tend to see God more likely in a balanced perception. There is no significant level between the A, B, or C groups.

Speaks of Christ as Lord and Savior. This category attempted to solicit from the interviewee the frequency of religious language, including concepts such as speaking of Christ as Lord and Savior. The data were grouped into three categories: not at all, seldom, and frequently. The specific data can be seen in Table 23.

There is clear evidence that the active church member speaks more frequently about Christ as Lord and Savior than does the less active or inactive member. The differeces are statistically significant between the A and B groups (.001 level) and the A and C groups (.001 level). The specifics are as follows in the not at all level: A — 32%, B — 88%, C — 74%. At the seldom level the As had 52%, the Bs 6%, and the Cs 5%. In the frequently category the As indicated a 16% response, while the Bs had 6%, and the Cs 17%. The Cs speak just as frequently about Christ as Lord as do the active members of the church. The Bs, on the other hand, have a large drop in their use of religious language with only 6% in the frequent category.

Familiar with church structure. Familiarity with the working structure of their local church and denomination was recorded in this sample and the results can be seen in Table 24. The population of this study was placed in three categories: not at all, moderate, great. The responses affirmed what was expected, in that the active member (A), would have more information and be more familiar with the church than those who were less active.

The statistics of their responses fell into the following categories. In the not at all category the As had 2%, Bs 18%, and Cs 17%. These figures indicated there is a significant difference between the As and the Bs (.05 level), and a significance level of .05 between the As and Cs. In the moderate category the As had 44%, the Bs 59%, with the Cs 43%. At this level there is relatively little difference between the groups, though the Bs are slightly higher. At the great level there is a larger variance. The As had 54%, the Bs 24%, and the Cs 39%. In general, the active church member has more familiarity with local church structure, as well as structures beyond the local church, than does the less active or inactive member.

Uses faith to help make decisions. Table 25 points out the statistics for using one's faith for making decisions. When talking about that issue with the interviewees, the interviewers noted the following:

Those who stated that they did not use their faith at all in making decisions fell in the following categories: A — 8%, B — 35%, and C — 22%. In the sometime group the As had 61%, the Bs 53%, and the Cs 57%. The frequently group indicated the As had 31%, the Bs 12%, and the Cs 21%. When comparing the As with the Bs, it should be noted that they are statistically different at the .005 level. While the As do not differ significantly from the Cs, there is a slight leaning toward the As using their faith more frequently in making decisions.

Sees self as a minister to serve others. In observing the responses in this category, it was found that there is no significance between the A, B, and C groups regarding how they see themselves as a minister to serve others. All groups had low frequencies in the not at all category (A — 5%, B — 13%, C — 9%), while they all exhibited their highest scores in the sometimes frequency with the As having 55%, the Bs 44%, and the Cs 70%. In the highest category, frequently, the groups again had similar percentages (A — 40%, B — 44%, C — 22%). These statistics indicate that there does not seem to be a shift or loss of the "minister" image as people move away from the life of the church.

Sees self as a recipient of church's services. The data gathered around this subject follows those areas of this study determined by the selection of the sample. It would seem reasonable to suppose that those who do not attend worship, give financially, or who have some major conflict with the pastor or another member, would also be the type of people who would not likely be recipients of the church's services. This proved to be true in this study. Table 27 delineates the responses. Those who received no services at all from the church are found predominantly in the B and C groups, (A — 17%, B — 47%, C — 57%). For those who answered that sometimes they received services of the church, the response is quite even (A — 46%, B — 47%, C — 35%). There is, however, variation at the frequency level of receiving the church's services. The As had the highest with 37%, the Bs with only 4%, and the Cs 7%. The data indicated that statistically there is a significant level (.01) between the As and Bs and .001 level between the As and Cs. The As receive the services of their church more frequently.

Sees the Bible as an important book. As the data above was significantly different between the As, Bs, and Cs, the data in Table 28 is also statistically significant. This category attempted to clarify if persons active in the church perceive the Bible as a more important book than those who are less active or inactive. Those who do not see the Bible as an important book were distributed as follows: A — 9%, B — 59%, C — 39%. In the sometimes groups the As had 42%, the Bs 12%, and the Cs 39%, while the frequently group indicated that the As had the highest response with 48%, the Bs with 24%, and the Cs with 22%. The As are significantly different than the Bs (.001 level), which indicates that the active member sees the Bible as a more important book than does the less active member. The As are also significantly different than the Cs at a .005 level of significance. These statistics suggest that close proximity to the community of faith stimulates continuity with the use of the Scriptures as an important and meaningful book.

List other religious ideations. This item in the research proved to be invalid. So few interviewers responded that the data were not sufficient to draw any conclusions.

Original Church Involvement

Responses from this sample indicated interesting reasons for joining the church. Because it was difficult to get statistical information, the data will be general. Though it was possible to plot some frequencies, the use of language of each interviewer makes a clear interpretation difficult.

Some of the general trends, those most often mentioned by active members for joining the church, are as follows. They are ranked according to frequency of response by the interviewer: like the minister, people were friendly, desired to serve others, felt needed, and joined as a child.

When comparing the above list with the Bs (less active) the order changes and new reasons are given: joined as a child, church close by, and friendly. There is no mention in the B group of a desire to serve others, nor did they feel that they were needed.

When looking at the response of the inactive group (C), the replies were very few. I recall in the many interviews which I personally secured that it was very difficult to get the people to talk about why they joined that congregation. They would immediately move to the more pressing subject of why they left; therefore, the data were not sufficient for any kind of ranking.

The Helpless-Hopeless Characteristics of These Persons

The major thesis of this book deals with the problems of dropping from an active church relationship to an inactive status. On route to the inactive position, these persons pass through feelings of helplessness (leading to apathy) and/or hopelessness (leading to boredom). We attempted to get data on those feelings and tried to distinguish if an individual was showing these affects according to the A, B, and C groupings. There were some striking differences between the As and the other groups.

The active persons in this sample showed a predominance of well integrated persons. That is, they did not show any distinctive characteristic which indicated that the person was either helpless or hopeless. Slightly over 60% of the As had no signs of helplessness or hopelessness, while 13% showed signs of helplessness and 10% exhibited evidence of hopelessness. (Helplessness is most easily seen in the external blame orientation to a given problem, while the hopeless person is more prone to blame himself or herself for the problem that had developed). Four percent of the sample exhibited evidence of both helplessness and hopelessness.

In contrast to the As, the Bs had a very different pattern of response. Only 19% of the Bs showed integration, while 50% felt helpless and 31% felt hopeless. No one exhibited feelings of both helplessness and hopelessness.

The Cs, on the other hand, showed a slightly different pattern than the Bs but considerable difference than the As. There was no sense of integration in any of the Cs (compared with B — 19%, A — 60%). This group displayed very strong and distinctive feelings of helplessness (66%) and hopelessness (33%). It is quite evident from these statistics that the further down the dropout track a person moves, the more clearly the affects of helplessness and hopelessness are exhibited. In essence, the Cs have reached the apathetic and bored positions; that is, they have fixed their blame orientation in terms of church involvement on either themselves or others and have remained stabilized in that position.

SUMMARY

In summarizing the above statistical work, it is possible to classify the differences between the active members of a congregation (A), those who have become less active (B), and those who have dropped out completely from all church relationships (C). The comparative study is intended to see the differences between the A and B groups and also the A and C groups. There are those areas of investigation which I thought might have proven significantly different, but did not.

They are summarized as follows:

Areas which did not prove to be significant between the A and B groups fall in the following subjects: financial giving, changes in frequency of worship, conflict with pastor, family income, occupation, education, church hopping, anxiety during the interview, conflict with church members, theological issues, financial issues, God seen as outside or inside of self, and sees self as minister to others.

The above items indicate there is no difference in the population between those who are active in the life of the church and those who are beginning to dropout. The areas which are significant, however, appeared as follows: age (Bs have older persons), serving on committees, worship attendance, ability to articulate one's faith, conflict with a family member, overworked, involvement in community (Bs more involved), God as active in the world, speaks of Christ as Lord, familiar with church structure, uses faith to make decisions, sees self as recipient of church's services, and the Bible as an important book.

These items illustrate those components which begin to change in the dropout pattern. That is, behaviors, feelings, attitudes, etc. begin to take on certain characteristics between the active and the less active persons. It should be noted that the As are taken as the norm, and when there is variance, it is away from the A behaviors. In a few cases, i.e., involvement in community activities, the Bs have a higher rate than the As. In such cases I will point out the shift in direction of the difference.

The following did not prove to be significant when comparing the active members (A) with the disinterested members (C). They are: age, family income, occupation, education, church hopping, anxiety during the interview, theological issues, educational issues, involvement in community, God as active in the world, God as seen outside or inside of self, uses faith to make decisions, and sees self as a minister to others.

There is a rather large number of studied categories between the As and Cs which did prove to be significant. They are: financial giving, serving on committees, worship attendance, change in frequency of worship, articulating one's faith, conflict with the pastor, conflict with other church members, conflict with family members, financial issues, overworked, speaks of Christ as Lord, familiar with church structure, sees self as recipient of church's services, and Bible as an important book. The disinterested (apathetic or bored) member gives less, serves on committees less, worships less, has a higher frequency of change in worship habits, is not able to articulate his or her faith as clearly (if at all), has considerably more conflict with the pastor, other church members, and his or her own family. The (C) group also has more conflict over financial issues and expresses the feeling of being overworked. They do not speak of Christ as Lord as frequently, are not as familiar with church structures, and do not see themselves as recipients of the church's services. They also hold the Bible as a less important book than do the active members.

Those areas in which *both* the B and C groups are different from the As fall into a different pattern. Both the B and C groups serve less on committees, worship less frequently, do not articulate their faith as clearly, have more conflict with their family members and other church members over church related issues, feel overworked, and speak less frequently of Christ as Lord. The B and C groups are less familiar with church structures, and see themselves as recipients of the church's services less frequently than the As. Finally, both B and C groups see the Bible as a less important book in their lives than the active church member.

Special attention is given to several characteristics which exist between the B and C groups, without reference to the As. A comparison between the B and C activity levels indicates that the Bs have an older group of persons (Table 3), give more financially (Table 8) and attend worship with more regularity (Table 10).

A special insight is found in Table 12 regarding the ability to articulate the Christian faith. There is a shift from less articulation (Bs — 5.8%) to more articulation (Cs — 23.1%). This indicates that when a person is moving away from the church one's religious language is suppressed. When the individual has completely dropped out, the member is able to recover some of the lost religious language. It is my suspicion that as the anxiety level increases with the B group, the thought of using religious language becomes less congruent than after the dropout has occurred.

In line with the above statistics, Table 21 (Responses to the Concept of Seeing God as Active in World) indicates a similar pattern. The Bs show less awareness of God's activity in the world than the Cs. As the church member becomes less active one becomes less aware of God's activity in the world. Only when the dropping-out has been completed is there a return to seeing God active in the world. Table 23 indicates the same trend (at the frequently level) in speaking of Christ as Lord and Savior, and Table 25 (Uses Faith to Help Make Decisions) follows the same pattern.

I do not think that these tables show this trend out of coincidence. They all affirm that when the individual is actively involved in the emotional work of dropping-out that the religious ideation follows the same pattern; namely, it drops out. This concept was affirmed many times in the interviews when the interviewer could readily note that when the person "fell apart," his or her theology was one of the segments of life that "fell."

Educational issues also show up as different between the B and C categories. The Bs have a considerably higher level of conflict over educational issues than do inactive persons. The data collected did not give any clues why this occurs and is something needing futher exploration.

This brief summary should help the reader formulate some of the differences between the active, less active, and inactive church member.

NOTES

[1] The statistical test used in this research is the Chi-square test which is a hypothesis-testing technique used to test (1) a set of observed frequencies with a set of hypothetical frequencies, (2) two or more sets of observed frequencies with the objective of finding out if the differences among the sets are significant. Since frequencies are the result of counting, the Chi-square test is applicable to data in discrete form. Statistical significance is set at .05. Robert D. Mason and Roger H. Hermanson, *Business and Economic Statistics* (Georgetown, Ontario: Learning Systems Company, Irwin-Dorsey Limited, 1970), p. 102.

[2] *The Times Union* (Rochester), February 3, 1975, p. 1-A, cols. 2-7.

Chapter 4

Questions and Answers on the Apathetic and Bored Church Member

INTRODUCTION

This chapter brings together the review of literature in Chapter 2 and data gathered in the research project in Chapter 3. I will answer the major questions asked in the opening chapter. These questions were: (1) What are the psychological and theological dynamics which occur in the life of a church member who is at one time active and two or three years later is inactive? (2) Where do the affects of apathy and boredom originate? (3) What are the behavioral differentiations that take place as a result of anxiety producing events? (4) Does the inactive church member feel helpless or hopeless? (5) Are there some precipitants which occur more frequently than others? (6) Do members leaving the church blame themselves, or is there outward blame toward the institutional church? How can this differentiation be determined? These questions will be the guidelines for this chapter.

Following the six questions I shall use the data collected in Chapter 3 to verify or deny the hypotheses referred to in Chapter 1. I shall conclude with a brief but systematic discussion of the entire movement of a person from an active to an inactive relationship in the church.

WHAT ARE THE PSYCHOLOGICAL AND THEOLOGICAL DYNAMICS WHICH OCCUR IN THE LIFE OF A CHURCH MEMBER WHO IS AT ONE TIME ACTIVE AND TWO OR THREE YEARS LATER IS INACTIVE?

The essence of this research comes to focus in the answer to this question.

The Psychological Dynamics

In the beginning movement away from an active church relationship, there is an incident which produces some kind of anxiety, making the individual feel very uncomfortable. It gives one a sense of being off-balance. The initial reaction to the anxiety is to find a comfortable state again.

As was pointed out in Chapter 1, anxiety is the affect produced by an arousal period of short or long duration when a person feels knocked off one's equilibrium (emotional or psychical or rational balance).[1] When a member of a local congregation is disturbed by an event that is emotional and anxiety provoking, the entire physical system reacts to alleviate the discomfort.

Part of the understanding of why anxiety comes to the fore is seen in the context of learning experiences from childhood to adulthood. Schmale points out that anxiety is "the first psychic awareness of discomfort and probably remains throughout life the first and immediate reaction to the perception of psychic tension in any situation."[2] When any stimuli comes that upsets the person, readjustment to normalcy is required.

Anxiety may come from a variety of settings and sources within the life of the church. The reviewed literature indicates there are at least four major precipitants to anxiety: reality—occurring in one's own personal history, oriented in reality, and therefore without delusionary components; neurotic—resulting from thought patterns not based on historical events, frequently delusional with little concrete reality; moral—conflict or dilemmatic perception between two kinds of behavior (being aware at a cognitive level what is expected while doing the opposite); existential—described in theological or philosophical language as the thought that some day you may not exist, and that even if you do exist, your life may be utterly meaningless.

These kinds of anxiety were noted in less active and inactive church members. Some were seen more clearly than others. Some persons had a combination of them, and, therefore, the interviewer had to sift them out. Ninety-five percent of the persons interviewed in the B and C groups could tell quite clearly what the event was, when it happened, and could express strong feelings about it.

One way of testing the concept of anxiety in this study was to see if the interviewers could note a difference in the anxiety levels between the A, B, and C groups. Would the C group show more anxiety than the A group during the interview? Table 7 shows a slightly higher, though not statistically significant, degree of anxiety in the C group. More anxiety was noted between the As and the Bs but not at a significant level.

The important factor in understanding anxiety in this study is found in the precipitants of this affect. What triggers off the anxiety, making the parishioner so uncomfortable that he or she becomes angry enough to leave the church? There appear to be three very significant precipitants that bring these feelings of anxiety. They are in the order of their intensity: (1) conflict with the pastor (.001 level of significance), (2) conflict with another family member (.025 level of significance), and (3) conflict with another church member (.025 level). In each of the above cases the anxiety is produced by unresolved personal conflict. The lack of resolution keeps anxiety high, generating anger and creating distance.

When anxiety reaches the stage of acute discomfort, the parishioner attempts to resolve these feelings. Resolution occurs by rationalizing what is going on or by confronting the person, organization, or situation. In its initial stages, the anxiety is indicated by verbal signs such as: "It's too much," "It's no use," "I can't take it anymore," "I give up," "Nobody cares anymore," etc. Such phrases indicate a person is quite anxious and moving away from the church. If these signals are not picked up and no one helps resolve the anxiety, the individual becomes angry. When the anger develops, the individual shows more agitated behavior, becoming more aggressive or withdrawn, either striking out at an individual or the institution or becoming depressed and blaming one's self for what has happened.

If the anger does not resolve the conflict, the resulting anxiety and pain will be too great to bear. If the individual finds no resolution to the anxiety and discovers that anger does not bring comfort or self-conquest of the problem, the anxiety is resolved by moving further away from the setting in which the stimuli is located. This is noted quite clearly in the frequency of worship, working on committees and financial giving. The comportment of the parishioner changes extensively and a reinvestment of time and money spent for the church changes significantly. Ninety-six percent of the As made a pledge to the church, while only 23% of the Cs pledged. This provides a significant difference at the .001 level (see Table 8). While 95% of the As served on committees, 100% of the Cs served on no committees. The Bs had 76% serving on no committees (see Table 9). Their behavior also changes in worship patterns with 88% of the A group attending 50% or more of the time, while 29% of the Bs and none of the Cs attend at the same frequency. Worship attendance is the first behavioral indicator of dropout and is one of the most sensitive indicators of what is happening to the parishioner.

These inactive members back off from their church relationships but do not re-engage in any other congregation. They are not church hoppers. Only one person fits that criterion out of the sample of 101 persons.

Each of the 23 persons interviewed in the non-active group indicated that no one from the church had ever come to find out why they were losing interest or had dropped out. It reinforced their belief that no one cared, and that they were not missed. One third of this group cried during the interview, indicating the intensity of unresolved feelings.

In many respects, anxiety that becomes anger also becomes a driver. That is, emotions become so strong they force the person to retreat in order to survive. In that case, the withdrawal, a type of conservation, allows the person to go on functioning in a fairly normal way.

When the individual begins to move away from the church, there is expressed a considerable amount of grief mixed with the anger. The church, for most of these non-actives, was a very important object in their lives. They still talk about it as being "their" church and "that minister (or other persons or situation) is there and they cannot return until he/it goes away." As the individual moves away, one feels the loss that comes from missing important relationships and experiences. It became quite apparent in the interviews that the move from an active relationship was accompanied with a strong sense of grief and a longing to return to a comfortable state.

At the time of the disengaging, anxiety and anger allow the person to reach out in an attempt to engage the church. Two dynamics are noted: (1) there is distance created, (2) there is an opportunity to find each other again and possibly punish the party that had made the individual feel so badly. In the punishment there is the hope that all those concerned with the loss will learn from it and therefore provide a situation that makes it less likely to occur again.[3]

For the C group, the learning that had taken place from their experiences seemed negligible. When asked in the interviews about the event that started them moving away from the church, they could respond quite clearly. But there was a strong feeling on the part of the interviewers that these persons could not get in touch with those feelings nor perceive why that event had caused the feelings that it did. They could readily express their anger but were not able to see that their inability to cope with their anxiety was part of their problem. It is as Sullivan says, "In somewhere around 94% of all occasions on which you are anxious, the security operations called out by the anxiety are the things you are perfectly clear on, whereas the precipitating anxiety is obscured."[4]

One powerful aspect about anxiety is that its "energy" can be used in a variety of ways. The "energy" can move the person toward creative resolution or to destructive relationships. Anxiety can be perceived as an alarm system.[5] The ringing of that alarm does not tell the person what to do or where to go when he or she gets anxious. It only makes the person aware that something is wrong and that action needs to be taken to set things right. For these (C) people the way to resolve the anxiety and turn off the alarm is to move away and suffer the ensuing loss. It is the price that one pays for returning to the comfortable state.

The Theological Dynamics

Prior to this project I saw persons who left the church as individuals who had forfeited their claim on the church and had sinned in the eyes of God. As a result of my research, I recognize that these individuals are aching, struggling, anxious persons who have great difficulty in living in an anxiety provoking setting. They are very different from what I had first suspected.

The following theological dynamics were sought from the sample: (1) the ability to articulate the Christian faith; (2) conflict with theological issues; (3) the belief that God is active in the world; (4) the seeing of God as outside or inside of self; (5) reference to Christ as Lord and Savior; (6) the use of faith to help make decisions; (7) the view of self as a minister to serve others; and (8) the function of the Bible as an important book in their lives.

Responses to these areas proved indicative of a change from active to inactive positions. What happens to the religious language of the person who begins to move away from the active church setting? There is a considerable loss of religious language (see Table 12). All of the active members were able to articulate their faith at a moderate or higher level, while the less active and inactive persons had more difficulty. The inactive group could articulate their faith better than the less active, but not as well as the active member. In interviewing these persons, it was my perception that the guilt, grief, shame, and blame orientation helped to suppress the ability to talk clearly about one's faith. It was apparent that they were unsure of their faith. The church was providing a difficult setting in which to live, and the ensuing disillusionment and anxiety challenged their faith.

Anxiety levels are precipitated primarily by rational problems and not theological ones. There were no significant differences between the active or inactive members regarding theological issues. This implied that persons did not leave the church because of conflict over diverse theological matters. This, I believe, holds true for the United Methodist Church in general. The United Methodists are very eclectic theologically and embrace a wide theological spectrum. In the "Doctrine and Doctrinal Statements" of the United Methodist Church it is stated that their doctrine allows for, ". . . indeed they positively encourage, variety in United Methodist theologizing."[6] This does not imply that there is no conflict, for approximately 20% of the sampled group reported moderate conflict over theological issues, but there is no significant difference between active and inactive members (see Table 16).

If there is no significant theological conflict, does the concept of seeing God as active in the world show any differentiation between the active and less active person? There does seem to be a major change in point of view about God's activity in the world as the person slides down the dropout track. It is shown in Table 21 that 48% of the active, 20% of the less active and 26% of the inactive express feelings strongly about God being highly active in the world. There is evidence that fewer persons in the less active group see God as active than in the other two. However, after the person had dropped out, there is a slight reorientation back to seeing God as active. There is a significant difference between the A and B groups at a .005 level, but there is no significance between the A and C groups.

An interpretation of this phenomenon can be given. After persons have dropped out, they wait 6-8 weeks to see if anyone will come to them to find out why they had left. During that period, there is a type of holding pattern—a nonengaging behavior—that takes place. They do not reinvest the time into any other area, but passively wait. When no help comes, they begin to reinvest their time in other organizations such as scouts, social service groups, etc., as well as recreational activities like camping. By the time they have reinvested their time much of the intense feeling has subsided, and a slight reorientation begins to take place toward how God works in the world. A phenomenon occurs: it is as if the parishioner equated God's ability to act in the world with one's own ability.

Several aspects that do not change with the dropout tracks are noted in Tables 22 and 26. The first table demonstrates that there are no distinctions between the A, B, and C groups regarding seeing God as outside or inside of themselves. This is to say that there is no significant difference. There is, however, a strong leaning away from a concept that God is in me, to that which is outside of me, as the persons disengage from close relationships in the church. The second table of how they saw themselves as ministers (Table 26) is somewhat surprising. Regardless of the group, they all saw themselves as ministers either sometimes or frequently (A — 95%, B — 88%, C — 92%). The difference came, not in their personal functioning as a "minister" of the Gospel, but the place of ministering. For the B and C groups it was primarily outside of the institution, while the A group did its ministering within the religious institution.

In several of the interviews it was noted that the C groups reported they saw themselves as active Christians, but the locale of their operation was no longer within the institutional church. These persons still maintain a Christian perspective in their life, although much of the religious piety drops away, i.e., their religious language, the use of the Scriptures, and using their faith to help make decisions (see Tables 23, 25, and 28). Because they have been hurt and made anxious by the persons within the institution, they move away from the church but do not seem to give up the central notion of being a Christian witness to the world. Their faith orientation shifts from serving the institutional church to serving persons outside of the institution. At least 50% of them still see themselves as servants of God (see Table 20).

When the anxiety provoking event occurs, there is an important twist that needs our consideration. There is a certain kind of pride that occurs in the A group, for they have not copped-out. Niebuhr argues that the most dangerous oar-resters are the good people, the free people, the

60

moral people, and the healthy people. They may find that their freedom leads them into the sin of pride, resulting, he says, in damage greater than in the case of the less good, the less free, the less moral, or the less healthy. "The better or freer or healthier a man is, the more it behooves him to have enough uneasiness so as not to become proud."[7]

This uneasiness Niebuhr calls anxiety. I did not sense any of this kind of uneasiness in the A group. To the contrary, it was noted that these persons felt that they were "in" and that kind of security produces a major problem. The "in" (active) group was not sensitive to the needs of those persons who were aching and leaving the church. That is why 100% of the C group could say, "No one ever came to visit me." The implications of that statement is that the A group did not sense the needs of those persons who were drifting away; who were, in fact, crying for help. The active member did not come to their aid. One of the major functions of this research is to sensitize the A group to the needs of the B and C groups, for each has a ministry to the other.

Part of the difficulty in training persons to confront the B and C groups is a feeling of being overwhelmed by the task. I have seen laypersons back off from the task because they did not want to become that sensitive to others, for it would provide too much pain for them personally. Kierkegaard describes this kind of anxiety as one standing on the edge of an abyss, the abyss of possibility. In this case, it is the abyss of helping other persons; the possibility is there, but when one looks into that chasm, the depth of responsibility becomes too anxiety provoking and the person retreats. It is in the retreating that we do not meet the responsibility and, therefore, do not serve the greatest creativity that is in us. Where then lies the problem? The fault is in the self's inability to sustain the pain of the dizziness, not the anxiety itself. The most difficult task of the active member dealing with the inactive is the self realization that there are forces that prevent the self from confronting one's responsibility to the inactive member.

What this leads to is a double barreled problem. The B and C groups do not face the anxiety of their own personal problems; that is, they do not engage the problem sufficiently to resolve it. On the other hand, those that do resolve it and remain active in the church find it difficult to sensitize themselves to work with the B and C groups. In many ways the issues are the same. This points out that we all have the feelings of anxiety and need to struggle with them. The capacity for feeling the dizziness is uniquely human. Our sin is that we retreat from the potential of possibility, for that is always a painful gaze into the abyss of our own lives.

WHERE DO THE AFFECTS OF APATHY
AND BOREDOM ORIGINATE?

The genetic beginnings of apathy and boredom occur in the first few months of life. In these early months the child's somatomotor organization develops, allowing it to follow, grasp, and bring objects to its mouth. When the child does this, it experiences pleasure and gratification. When, however, the infant does not experience this, it experiences displeasure and dissatisfaction. The child, at this stage, does not yet differentiate these objects from himself or herself, but perceives them as one with him or her. When gratification is not produced as expected, the child may then feel what later will be more clearly perceived as anxiety and anger. These disturbing feelings lead the child to a greater searching or reaching out to re-establish or find again specific gratification previously experienced. Thus, "anger reflects an intrapsychic awareness of fantasied object-activity. The affect of anger may reappear whenever an object-directed activity does not produce the expected results."[8]

When the adult reaches out for help (gratification) and does not receive it, the individual begins to feel the anxiety (discomfort), which in turn leads the person to reach out in order to get the satisfaction needed. When this does not occur, the child-adult will engage his or her environment vigorously (angrily) in order to persuade, manipulate, or control the possible outcome of the situation to his or her own benefit. When engaging the object-person does not bring results, the feeling of helplessness occurs. Thus, there is the awareness that the environment is deficient and not able to give the required help.

. . . a feeling of being deprived, let down or left out which was perceived as coming from a change in a relationship about which the individual felt powerless to do anything. The gratification which was lost was something the individual felt he could not go on without. Thus, he had to wait for its return, which for him usually meant the return of a highly valued object in the external world to provide the gratification desired.[9]

By eight months the child becomes very aware of the presence or absence of the parent and begins to struggle with the moments of separation. If the child can tolerate the absence of his or her parents (mothering figures) during this period, even if at times by the means of denial, he or she will begin to master the feelings of helplessness through an active exploration and engagement with other objects outside of one's self.

It is this basic feeling of helplessness that is taken into older childhood, youth, and adult years. It is this helpless feeling that leads to apathy. Apathy, therefore, is the feeling that nothing in my environment can come to my aid. As helplessness is the time of giving-up, apathy is the stage of having given-up. The person no longer engages the environment and, therefore, does not ask for help. This became very evident where 57% of the inactive group did not call on the church for its services, while only 17% of the active members did not ask for some kind of help from the church group (see Table 27).

Those early childhood feelings of helplessness get verified or denied many times throughout life. We have to give up many things and persons. Each time that is required we touch those helpless feelings. Frequently, the setting is more anxiety provoking than our ability to cope with it, and we move away from the situation for self preservation. When the mind becomes aware of possible self depletion of resources, it withdraws from the setting where the anxiety and danger are produced in order to re-establish a sense of equilibrium.

The person leaving the church, as a result of an anxiety setting, is acknowledging that he or she cannot cope with the amount of anxiety being produced and moves to another vantage point where life can go on with some kind of normalcy. In many cases the environment (church) did not respond to the call for help, and the individual retreated from a depleted source of staying power. He or she dropped out to save himself or herself.

As the apathetic person is not able to find help from the outside world to solve his or her problem, the bored person comes to the point of dropping out because of a lack of inner resources. The phenomenon occurs first in the child between the ages of three and six. This stage involves the sensitive period of infantile sexual role differentiation. The child soon discovers that regardless of how hard he or she tries, he or she cannot succeed in being the preferred object over the parent. That is, the child cannot have the chosen parent for his or her "mate." The capacity to tolerate this perception is "aided by the psychic defense of repression which allows the child to enter latency where he has a great spurt in intellectual development without the continued awareness of feeling inadequate." (Erikson's periods of initiative and industry).[10]

When the child realizes (sometimes unconsciously) that he or she cannot succeed, feelings of unworthiness, guilt, shame, and hopelessness arise. These are intensified through the growing years by other experiences. They are either dealt with creatively and foster the ability of the child, or they can be used to defeat the goals that the child wants to achieve. If the child finds that his or her feeling of unworthiness is confirmed in other ways, the feeling is strengthened and becomes part of the personality structure taken into the teen and adult years. When this phenomenon occurs in the adult, the individual will tend to withdraw from one's relationships with others and blame one's self. When an anxiety setting is encountered and one is not able to cope with these strong feelings, the adult will move away by turning the anger on himself or herself, feel guilty, and quietly leave the church. These feelings produce a sense of hopelessness and ultimately boredom. Bored adults are those who have poor self images and tend to punish themselves for anything that goes wrong. They do not engage the outer world as does the helpless oriented person. Bored persons feel the church would not accept their angry behavior. These persons slip from the church membership without any noise and fade away without anyone's noticing. When this occurs, it becomes even more evident to them that they are worthless because no one even misses them.

The affects of helplessness-hopelessness and the resulting apathy-boredom tracks become differentiated in the adult. The research data indicates the C group was far more inclined to be either apathetic or bored. What is quite striking is that when the person has become a dropout, it is quite easy to determine if the individual is either apathetic or bored.

WHAT ARE THE BEHAVIORAL DIFFERENTIATIONS THAT TAKE PLACE AS A RESULT OF ANXIETY PRODUCING EVENTS?

This question is answered, in part, by the previous questions but further elaboration is needed. Given a certain event in the life of the church which creates conflict and anxiety, the church population will tend to group themselves in four types of behaviors (only three groups are studied in my research). The first group works through the conflict and uses it to its own personal and group's advantage. They remain active in the life of the church. A second group falls in the helpless-apathetic grouping. They blame the external world via the institution or persons in it. If these people do not resolve the conflict, they move down the dropout track until they become apathetic. At this point they have completely withdrawn from the active life of the church but still remain on the church rolls. A third group will behave like the apathetic group, but the blame orientation will be directed toward themselves. The outward behavior of both apathetic and bored persons will look alike in the sense of their moving away, but the direction of their blame will be opposite.

A fourth group, not considered in this study, is composed of those persons who, when angry, move down one of the two tracks (apathetic or bored), but do not become immobilized. These individuals leave the church institution and find another congregation more comfortable. One of the unique characteristics about apathetic and bored persons is that they do not change their setting, but remain in their local church membership even though they are inactive.

Why this differentiation between the groups? There appears to be a clear rationale for the difference.

As persons grow, they learn by trial and error what works best for them in the situation in which they live. When persons do not learn to cope with their early childhood tasks of relating and working through their conflictual feelings, they are prone to withdraw from the setting rather than engage it. Those persons that remain active in the church for many years are those persons who have learned to live in a variety of anxiety provoking settings successfully. I recall one interview with an older member who said, "I have learned to work in every church I have ever been a member, and I learned how to get along with the minister." She was 83 years old and still very active in church activities.

DOES THE INACTIVE CHURCH MEMBER FEEL HELPLESS OR HOPELESS?

A common problem of apathetic or bored persons is the inability to cope in a setting of high anxiety. They use apathy or boredom as a way of surviving under stress or conflict, even if it means isolation.

Apathetic prone persons engage the environment with vigor, attacking it and making every attempt to "make things right." When this does not occur, the feeling of helplessness (less-help) occurs and they begin to give up. In contrast, bored persons' blame orientation is directed toward the self. In extreme form these persons realize there is nothing they can do, no power they can exercise, no internal resource available and no way of altering the external condition through internal contrivance or manipulation. At this point bored persons become hopeless. Boredom is:

. . . a feeling of frustration, despair or futility perceived as coming from a loss of satisfaction for which the individual himself assumed complete and final responsibility and nothing more could be done that would undo the failure.[11]

The basic difference is the orientation or the direction of the anger. As Schmale puts it, "These two feelings represent two distinct and separate ways in which individuals feel themselves unable to cope or find a solution to a perceived loss of desired gratification and thus, experience giving-up."[12]

My research shows clear evidence that there is a distinct shift in the helpless-hopeless orientation as the individuals move further and further from the center of church activity. Sixty percent of the active church members show no evidence of being helpless or hopeless; 13% exhibited feelings of helplessness; 10% showed feelings of hopelessness; 4% expressed both helpless and hopeless feelings and the remaining 13% of the active members showed no response.

When we consider the results of the persons who are in the process of moving away from the church (B group), there is a very different pattern in the response. Only 19% of the Bs showed integration of their feelings, while 50% felt helpless and 31% felt hopeless. No one exhibited feelings of both helplessness and hopelessness.

With the inactive group, the tracks of apathy and boredom reach completion. No one in this group had integrated the two feelings. To the contrary, the group displayed very strong and distinctive feelings of helplessness. These persons became the apathetic population of the inactive group. On the other hand, 33% of the group fell in the hopelessness category and ended as bored church members. Twice as many persons in the group tended to be outward blame (helpless) oriented.

These figures show that the further down the dropout track persons travel, the clearer becomes the orientation of their blame and the intensity of their difficulty. There is a very clear difference between the A group and the B and C populations. Long term active church members are able to cope and integrate the feelings of helplessness and hopelessness. They are able to use their anxiety and anger in a way which does not drive them from their relations with other active church members.

ARE THERE SOME PRECIPITANTS WHICH OCCUR MORE FREQUENTLY THAN OTHERS?

Yes. This question will be answered by looking at those factors which occur with more intensity than others and provide the setting in which conflict and anxiety predominate.

There are precipitants which create a setting of anxiety and produce reactions that can be differentiated between the A, B, and C groups.

The greatest conflict falls within the inactive group (C). These persons have considerable conflict with the pastor, other church members, and interfamily members. All three of these conflict situations are statistically significant when compared with active church members. For example, only 4.2% of the active church members show a high level of conflict with the pastor, while 45.5% of the inactive persons expressed such conflict. [13]

An active member of the church may experience one or several of these anxiety experiences. When a multiple conflict occurs, the anxiety level rises higher and more rapidly.

An illustration from one of the interviews may help to clarify this phenomenon.

A young couple had been very active for over three years. They held major positions and fulfilled responsibility with enthusiasm. They arranged a family retreat for the entire church and were picked up by the pastor to travel to the retreat site. During the journey to the camp, the layperson told the pastor that he was not happy with the hymns the pastor selected for worship. The pastor did not respond to his request, and the layperson felt the minister did not listen to what he was saying. This made the layperson feel uncomfortable, and he began to question other aspects of the pastor's ministerial functions. During the interview, after talking about the car ride to camp, the layperson said, "I began to realize that his sermons weren't very good either." He then began to attend worship services less regularly.

His wife was very active in the church school, attending training and other business meetings. She told the interviewer that her husband put pressure on her to drop her church school activity because he had to babysit. This created enough conflict in their marriage to warrant dropping her church school work. In the meantime, a member of the church called during the church's financial drive and raised their anxiety more by his approach. By the end of the interview, it became quite apparent to the interviewer that all three elements (conflicts with pastor, mate, and other church members) were at work.

Two other characteristics were evident in this interview. The husband was externally blame oriented and showed evidence of being apathetic. He never talked about himself, only about the pastor and "those people up there." His wife, on the other hand, was expressing guilty feelings about dropping out, but felt hopeless about doing anything or she would be in severe conflict with her husband. She clearly showed boredom characteristics. The husband was blaming the external world while his wife was blaming herself.

Other issues which were characteristic of the C group were their conflict over financial issues and the feeling of being overworked in the life of the church. They had feelings of being "burned out." While 47% of the inactive group felt they were overworked, only 18% of the active members felt the same (see Table 19).

A special problem arises around conflict over financial issues. Table 17 shows that only 2% of the active members had a moderate or higher level of conflict, while the inactive members had 30%. There is strong evidence that this is a biased statistic. One of the churches in the sample had a very serious conflict over money matters and provided over 90% of the responses. The other three congregations expressed very little concern over financial matters. For those persons who had financial difficulties, a great deal of anger was expressed.

In summary: conflict with the pastor, with other church members, and with members of one's family are the situations around which most anxiety is stimulated, resulting in people leaving the congregation.

67

DO MEMBERS LEAVING THE CHURCH BLAME THEMSELVES, OR IS THERE OUTWARD BLAME TOWARD THE INSTITUTIONAL CHURCH? HOW CAN THIS DIFFERENTIATION BE DETERMINED?

When individuals are made anxious by some provoking event, they frequently act to resolve the issue and return to a normal relationship or personal sense of well-being. When this does not occur, active church members seek to fix the blame for their difficulties. For those persons who are apathetic prone, the direction of their blame will be external. They will attack the environment and hope to change it sufficiently so they can live more comfortably. Most laypersons who have been trained in the methods mentioned in Chapter 5 can soon differentiate between outward blame and inward blame persons. There are, however, those persons who will exhibit feelings of both (only 4% of this sample).

Outward blame oriented persons rarely use "I" statements. Instead they will use "they," "those," "that church," "that clique," etc. The inward blame directed person will use almost exclusively "I" statements; "I am to blame," "I did not do the job well enough," "I do not understand the minister's sermons," "I am not good enough to serve on the education committee," etc. "Me" and "my" statements will also be made by the bored person, i.e., "If it wasn't for me the committee would have done a better job," or "It's my fault that the finance drive did not reach its goal."

It is not difficult to sift from the language of the person interviewed the orientation of blame. Usually, within fifteen minutes into the interview the language will become clear as to what direction the person is headed.

THE DROPOUT TRACKS

The reader will find a dropout chart (page 70) which shows in graphic form the stages of the A, B, and C groups as they move from an active relationship with the church to complete disinterest.

The track always begins with some anxiety provoking event. The events are usually triggered by personal relationships, i.e., the pastor, another church member, or a member of the family. These events may be perceived as being reality, neurotic, or morally based. They may also show evidence of being existential in their structure.

When the anxiety level becomes too great to tolerate, active church members will give verbal signals for others to hear. If there is no response, the signals will come in the form of anger. Those persons who express their anger at others move down the apathetic track, while those expressing feelings of inward blame and guilt will progress down the bored track. As long as there is a chance for resolution of the anxiety

68

and anger, persons will remain active. When there is no resolution and the anxiety-anger levels become too great to tolerate, active church members will change their behavior patterns. This is noted in worship attendance, committee meetings, and dropping out of religious language. These behaviors become another clue to the community with hope that someone will notice that they are extracting themselves from the church.

During this period of moving away, persons experience grief at giving up favorite loved persons and objects. They experience the giving-up complex and suffer from a sense of loss and self-gratification. Unless someone comes to their aid and lets them talk about what is happening to them, they will continue down the track to the complete dropout level.

After a decision on their part to drop out has been made (it is not always a conscious decision), they will wait six to eight weeks before re-engaging their time that had previously been spent in church activities. This period of "limbo" serves two functions: to get in control of the loss they have suffered and to see if anyone from the church will come and talk with them. If no one from the church attends to their needs, they will re-engage their time and energy in other pursuits. About half of them will find other activities in the community to which they may give themselves. The other half will drop from all outside activities and devote themselves to their families, homes, sports, etc.

When re-engaging has been completed, persons have reached the bottom of one of the two tracks. If in beginning to drop out they tended to blame themselves for what has happened in their lives, they would have followed the track of boredom. If they orient their blame to the outside world of persons and institutions, they have become apathetic.

CONFIRMING OR NOT CONFIRMING THE HYPOTHESES OF THE APATHETIC AND BORED CHURCH MEMBER

Hypotheses 1-5 were confirmed (see page 8). The hypothesis (6) that age, occupation, and educational level would be significant factors in the disinterested church member did not prove valid.

Hypothesis 7 reads as follows: The institutional structure of the church has a direct effect upon the behavior of persons who move from an active to inactive status. This hypothesis was not met. Several persons felt their problems were a result of actions taken by the hierarchy of the United Methodist Church. This was only an issue in one of the churches and was not mentioned by the other three. There are implications that the church is structured in a way that persons are over-worked, but this was too vague to make this hypothesis valid. Until further study is completed, this hypothesis remains unmet.

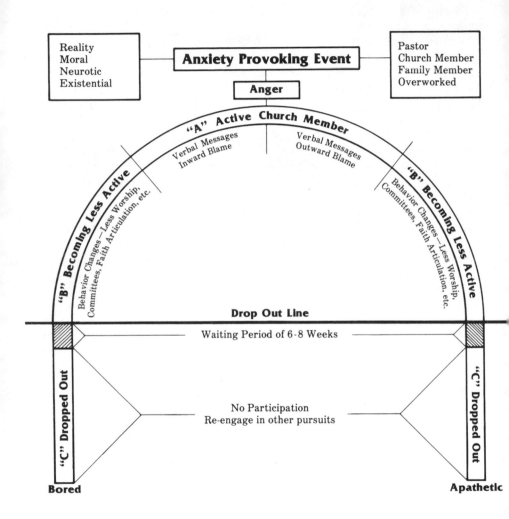

Reality
Moral
Neurotic
Existential

Anxiety Provoking Event

Pastor
Church Member
Family Member
Overworked

Anger

"A" Active Church Member

Verbal Messages
Inward Blame

Verbal Messages
Outward Blame

"B" Becoming Less Active

Behavior Changes—Less Worship,
Committees, Faith Articulation, etc.

"B" Becoming Less Active

Behavior Changes—Less Worship,
Committees, Faith Articulation, etc.

Drop Out Line

Waiting Period of 6-8 Weeks

No Participation
Re-engage in other pursuits

"C" Dropped Out

"C" Dropped Out

Bored

Apathetic

THE NEED FOR FURTHER RESEARCH

There are several major problems with this research, including the need to have a larger sample. It would be necessary to test the same hypotheses in other denominations and interdenominationally. Questions which go unanswered are: Would these results be the same for a group of rural churches or inner-city churches? Because the United Methodist Church is theologically eclectic, do dropouts occur more frequently than in conservative sects or fundamentalist churches? Would persons track in the same way as did these United Methodists?

A final need is to follow up on the training described in Chapter 5. Does the methodology work? Do persons change their feelings and behaviors as a result of a resolution procedure, or do their relationships become more distant from the church? Only further study will bring answers to these questions.

NOTES

[1] Albert Bandura, *Aggression: A Social Learning Analysis* (Englewood Cliffs, N.J.: Prentice Hall, 1973), p. 54.

[2] Arthur H. Schmale, Jr., "A Genetic View of Affects," *The Psychoanalytical Study of the Child*, Vol. XIX (1964), p. 290.

[3] John Bowlby, "Processes of Mourning," *International Journal of Psychoanalysis* (1961), Vol. 62, p. 317.

[4] Harry Stack Sullivan, *The Psychiatric Interview* (New York: W. W. Norton & Company, Inc., 1970), p. 60.

[5] Seward Hiltner and Karl Menninger (eds.), *Constructive Aspects of Anxiety* (New York: Abingdon Press, 1963), p. 26.

[6] *The Book of Discipline of the United Methodist Church*, The United Methodist Publishing House, 1972, p. 75.

[7] Reinhold Niebuhr, *The Nature and Destiny of Man: A Christian Interpretation* (New York: Charles Scribner & Sons, 1941), Vol. VII.

[8] Schmale, "Genetic View," p. 289.

[9] A. H. Schmale, "Giving Up as a Final Common Pathway to Changes in Health," *Adv. Psychosomatic Medicine*, Vol. 8, pp. 20-40.

[10] Schmale, "Final Common Pathway," p. 24.

[11] Schmale, "Final Common Pathway," p. 23.

[12] Schmale, "Final Common Pathway," p. 23.

[13] An interesting study of counter transference with the pastor can be found in Donald S. Williamson's, "A Study of Selective Inhibition of Aggression by Church Members," *The Journal of Pastoral Care*, Vol. XXI (Dec. 1967) No. 4, pp. 193-208.

Chapter 5

Visitation and Planning Methods for Encountering the Apathetic and Bored Church Member

INTRODUCTION

This chapter shall consider methods for training clergy and laity in encountering the apathetic and bored church member. The methods described below come from a variety of fields, i.e., organizational development, human relations training, encounter groups, consultation skills, etc.

I shall also develop a systematic view of visitation techniques which will include diagnosis (determining the degree of apathy or boredom) and an action plan for follow-through.

TRAINING THE CLERGY AND LAITY

Both clergy and laity are to be involved in visitation and should be trained. The function and purpose of calling on another member of a congregation is to provide meaningful contact in a ministry of caring, enabling both caller and callee to develop their human responsibility to each other and to the God in Christ to whom they both belong. The function is never to be manipulative, judgmental, nor demeaning, but supportive, encouraging, and upbuilding. These basic characteristics of the calling ministry are for the purpose of sharing the redeeming love of God.

The Methodology

The following methodologies have been created through experimental training of lay and clergy persons. The training occurred at local, district, conference, and national levels. In these experiences the response to the training has been both positive and fruitful.

A more meaningful experience occurs when two or more persons from a church or organization attend a given workshop. When experiencing similar activities, these persons relate more easily to each other and return to the local congregation with mutual support.

In the training and administrative procedures which follow I am assuming a pastor (male) will act as trainer.

His first task is to select a calling team consisting of men and women of various ages. After selecting and recruiting these persons (see below for recruiting principles), a time is set for training.

The first training task is orientation and contract building. Orientation is a process by which all persons know the goal and intent of the training. They are there to learn evangelistic visitation skills—to practice and develop them. The orientation should include the number of training sessions that are needed, times and dates, plus the required number of visitations. Once the orientation has been completed, it is necessary to contract with the callers.

One type of contract is a written statement presented to the individuals during the orientation. In signing the contract, the individuals would commit themselves to a common agreement. Another form of contracting is to verbally agree with each other regarding training and visitation.

Other issues may arise while contract building as the implications of committing one's self for a designated time is frequently problematic. Once the caller begins to make calls into the home, the need for continued training in other disciplines becomes greater. Need for training in theology, the Bible, church history, and church administration may be acknowledged and required.

After orientation and contracting, it is necessary to build a calling team which will bring strength and guidance to its members. Assuming the callers do not know each other, it is necessary to provide a process by which they become acquainted. The following team-building exercises are suggested.

If at least twelve persons are participating, ask each member in the group to choose someone that he or she knows the least. When all partners have been chosen, ask them to select two other couples with which they would like to work, thus making groups of six.

Once the teams have been selected, they are instructed to sit in chairs around a table. The trainer asks each member of the teams to take Form A (previously passed out to them). Form A consists of four open-ended statements which are: My name is . . . . , My immediate family includes . . . . , Other jobs I hold in the local church are . . . . , My occupation is . . . . . The instructions for the use of this sheet are as follows: "Would you please take Form A and, going around your group, share the open-ended statements with the rest of the members." If the persons on your working teams are familiar with each other, this form can be changed to get at deeper issues and can be revised accordingly. Under normal circumstances, approximately three minutes are given to a group of six to accomplish the task.

Next, Form B is given to the group. This form consists of open-ended questions of a more personal nature. It, along with Form A, can be found in the appendix, and can be copied for distribution to the training members. The questions are: What I am proud about in my church is . . . . , When someone asks me to call on an angry church member I feel . . . . , The thing I like most about myself is . . . . , I am happiest when . . . . .

The instructions for this form are as follows: Each person in the group of six is asked to answer one or more of these questions in a two-minute period. At the end of two minutes, he or she will pass to a neighboring person, who will also respond. The trainer will indicate when the two minutes are up and the persons can continue to move around the group. Form B gets at deeper personal issues.

Upon completion of this exercise, the trainer will point out to the callers that visitation evangelism is rooted in developing meaningful relationships. If a meaningful relationship cannot be established between the caller and the callee, it is quite certain that the Gospel of Christ will not be received with much enthusiasm.

These team-building exercises can be accomplished in a variety of settings and in a number of training sessions. They can be developed and administered in one day or over a period of weeks. The procedures described here are designed for a series of sessions that total at least five hours. Certain aspects can be shortened to reduce it to three hours if the trainer desires. This would only be introductory. Depth procedures take a minimum of twenty to thirty hours of training, usually over a ten to fifteen week period.

One fun team-building process is as follows: Take a large box of tinker toys and divide them in half. Put each half in a large ziploc bag and give them to the teams of people. (You will need one bag or half a box of tinker toys for each team of six persons.) Give the following directions: "This exercise will take fifteen minutes, divided into three five-minute segments. The first stage is to design on paper the tallest, strongest structure you can build with the tinker toys. You may investigate the items in the bag, but do not take them out of their container. After discussion, design the strongest and tallest structure you can create. You will have five minutes to design, in cooperation with each other, what you will later try to build."

After taking five minutes for designing, instruct the groups to take the tinker toys from the bags and build the structure without using verbal communication. They can communicate in any other form, including writing, but they may not speak to each other. They will have five minutes in which to build the tower.

At the end of five minutes they are to discuss the following: Did you build what you designed? What kind of feelings did you have about your team; that is, was each member of the team an active participant or did some sit back and watch, while others did the work? What did it feel like to be a member of that team? Were you supportive of each other? When this discussion is finished (five minutes), they are ready for the next stage. The tinker toy structures can be retained on a table as a symbol of their common work together. (Another alternative to the tower design is to ask participants to create a Christian symbol that reflects their unity or diversity.)

The next stage of training develops the process of listening skills. The following procedure is suggested.

The trainees are in groups of six. Each person is given paper and pencil and asked to write the three most important reasons why persons are not involved in the church. Though this content, in and of itself, may be important, it becomes a vehicle through which the listening experience can take place.

After the trainees have written their reasons, they are asked to form dyads with a member of their group. These persons will share their three responses and come to a consensus on three of the six. They will have five minutes to accomplish this and return to their original sextet. Next they get a consensus on the three groups of three items as it comes from the dyads.

After five to ten minutes of discussion, the trainer will interrupt this process to introduce new ground rules. The ground rules are: No person may speak in the group until he or she has paraphrased what the person prior to him or her has said. Paraphrasing is the process of repeating back to the individual who has just spoken what the listener thought he or she has said. The listener checks what the speaker said to see if his or her message is correctly perceived. This form of listening shows concern for the speaker. There is a basic understanding in this process; unless you are willing to listen to the other person, it is fairly certain that he or she won't be willing to listen to you.

In addition to paraphrasing, there are three other active listening skills. These are checking for feelings, clarifying, and questioning.

Clarifying is the process occurring during the paraphrasing stage when repetitions of thoughts were given back to the speaker. This is frequently done when a question is asked to verify the speaker's statement. When these four active listening components are developed, the group will listen more intently to one another.

This procedure will slow the group's discussion. It also may produce frustration and an attempt to subvert the task may be noted. To make sure this does not take place, instruct the group to police itself. If someone begins to speak without actively listening, members of the group should stop that person and ask him or her to paraphrase, thus not undercutting the learning potential. When this new ground rule is given to the group, the process is usually extended for ten to fifteen minutes to allow each group member to take part in this listening process. When the practice session has ended, it is important to get feedback from the groups, discussing the difficulty and effectiveness of the procedure.

Another method for developing listening skills is through a triad

75

practice. The group of six persons is divided into two groups of three. Each person is asked to choose a number—one, two or three. When the numbers have been assigned, the trainer writes three words on a flip-over chart or blackboard: (1) speaker, (2) listener, (3) coach. The following instructions are given: For a period of two minutes the speaker will talk to the listener, answering the open-ended question (What troubles me most as a caller is . . . .). The listener actively listens. He or she does not give advice nor share his or her own experiences. The listener uses paraphrasing, checking for feelings, clarifying, and questioning as his or her approach to the speaker. The third person, the coach, observes what is happening and interrupts if he or she perceives something is being misunderstood. If there is good communication between the speaker and the listener, the coach will sit passively and not enter into the discussion.

At the end of the two-minute period the roles are changed, and number one becomes the listener, number two the coach, and number three the speaker. In a period of six minutes each member of the triad will have an opportunity to speak, listen, and act as coach. This procedure allows intesive analysis of the process. When the six-minute period is completed, an additional three to five minutes are allowed to discuss the process and share experiences. With the above procedures practiced, it is then feasible to role-play a call.

The practice call has several stages. A team of six persons is divided into three groups of two. Each team member is given a number—one, two, or three. When the numbers have been selected, a task is given to each dyad. Team number one will be callers, team two callees, and team three observers. The *callers* are assigned a specific role, such as calling on an apathetic or bored member. The *callees* are told what kind of call this will be and are responsible for role-playing that behavior. The *observer* will be responsible for observing the transaction and noting the listening skills described above.

Each team of two persons is given five minutes to plan its procedures. After the five minutes they return to their group to practice the call. The process develops a feeling for calling in a variety of situations. Errors can be made in the call without any grave results. Each member of the team is encouraged to take the role as caller, as well as the other positions. The role-playing process has profound effects upon the caller and will produce effective simulation for actual calls. When the simulation calls are completed, the group of six persons gathers for a debriefing. Learning takes place through critiquing, thus helping to set the agenda for later training events.

After the above procedures, the caller can make his or her first parish visit. Visiting is frequently accomplished in teams of two. One good characteristic of the two person team is the ability to critique the visit with the calling partner.

76

An excellent procedure in training an unskilled layperson is to work with a skilled caller. The two by two process can be utilized until the training has been developed; then each individual can make his or her calls alone.

Training the Clergy

The following procedures assume that the pastor is making a call on his or her own people, that he or she is doing it alone, and that the calls are on less interested or disinterested members. These persons are described in this book as B and C categories.

The pastor calls on a variety of people for many reasons, including potential new members, those confined to their homes, laypeople on committees, etc. The training needed for calling on apathetic and bored members is of a different nature. Frequently the pastor is seen as a community of one, and what he or she does or doesn't do influences the entire parish. This is important because as the pastor comes to a bored or apathetic member he or she comes as a caring person, bringing an understanding of the reconciling love of Jesus Christ. Before the pastor can enter into that kind of relationship, it is necessary that he or she be trained effectively for these types of calls.

Within the United Methodist Church there is a concept of "clusters," where a number of churches gather in common ministry within a regional or geographical area. This generally consists of seven, eight, or nine congregations in which pastors and laity join in training events and other effective ministries. These events can provide adequate opportunity for learning the skills necessary to confront the apathetic and bored member. The following suggests several approaches that can be made in these visits.

I believe it very important for a pastor to call on the apathetic or bored parishioner only by appointment. There are exceptions to this, as determined by the traditions of a given parish. In my own experience in a suburban church, I have found appointments necessary, saving time and allowing preparation on the part of the callee.

There are several ways to make the initial contact. The pastor can contact the callee, setting the time and place. In that phone call there would be an opportunity to sense the feelings of the people and to deal directly with the possibility of being turned down. If there is refusal of the visit, it may be necessary for the pastor, while speaking on the telephone, to identify some of the problems the parishioner is having. Comments such as, "I sense that my call in your home would be very uncomfortable for you," help clarify anxious feelings. This procedure checks out feelings and frequently opens further discussion. Assuming the call is agreed upon, the pastor can make the appointment for his visit.

Preparation for a visit should be as extensive as possible. The pastor needs to know as much about the parishioner as he or she can discover. This includes checking church attendance records, noting family participation in church related activities such as committees, youth work, choir, church school, etc. Frequently, it is possible to get data from other members of the church. This information should be used with caution, as it may contain more rumor than fact. The pastor should not make his call on the inactive parishioner until all available information has been secured.

Before any further discussion on the call to the apathetic or bored member, I will survey the training possibilities for pastors at the district level. Each denomination has its own criteria for levels of ministerial organizations. The task is to bring pastors and laypeople together who wish to learn visitation skills regardless of whether it is a designated structure of a specific denomination or a similar organization binding clergy and laypersons in a common bond.

Clergy in communities where there are institutions of higher education may secure resource persons in the fields of psychology, theology, sociology, and philosophy. All of these disciplines can and do impinge upon the calling process. None of these professionals will necessarily be skilled in the visitation process but can provide the pastoral group with background information necessary for understanding the calling task. Literature and data found in this research project would also be used in visitation training.

I have found three general approaches to be very effective in training clergy at the district level. Pastors might gather for a two or three hour workshop, dealing minimally with the processes of team building, active listening skills, and role playing.

A more extensive training program at the district level would be a one day training session, lasting approximately nine hours. At this workshop an individual can be exposed to a considerable amount of experience and data in a short period of time.

Another effective method of training is for a group of pastors to meet over a number of weeks. A trainer would meet with them on a weekly basis to critique each of their calls and do a case study on each of the parishioners. This approach is, by far, the most efficient and meaningful in training clergy and is encouraged by this writer.

The character of training begins to change at regional or national levels of a given denomination because of excessive distance and cost of travel. A basic procedure is suggested: hold a week or weekend laboratory training event in a local church with the congregation being host. The pastor would invite a group of pastors from his or her state or neighboring states.

The week of training begins with team building processes. The first two days are spent in developing calling skills without being directly involved with parishioners. The rest of the week is spent in numerous calls to members of the local parishes who have been selected and previously contacted for appointments. Study in the areas of scripture, theology, behavioral psychology, and sociology would be appropriate. A staff of persons from that specific denomination, or from other communities, could be invited to participate in the training procedures. Costs could be defrayed through registration fees or subsidized by denominations or foundations. The provision for the best leadership available is of key importance for these conferences. Leadership can be provided through the executives of the departments of evangelism of most denominations, and also through highly skilled human relations trainers. Your denominational leaders can help you find these persons.

Training the Laity

The previous section emphasized the importance of the pastor being trained in order to encourage his or her people. I cannot emphasize enough the importance of training laity. I do not believe that the clergy-person in any congregation can sufficiently do the task needed without lay help. This not only involves the concept of effective use of laypeople in the church, but it also has direct implication that all members of the Christian Church are ministers and have certain pastoral functions to perform for each other. A distinctive element in the research was the feeling of abandonment on the part of the apathetic and bored members when no one from the church made any attempt to contact them. My experience indicates that many of them would have responded with eagerness if someone in the parish had shown concern. I remember one interviewee's saying to me, "I have not been active in my church for ten years, and no one has ever asked me why." This individual did not indicate whether that person should have been the pastor or a layperson. The only thing she was concerned about was whether members of the church cared.

In most congregations, apathetic and bored members number about one third of their memberships. It is not feasible for the pastor to make contact with all these persons. Therefore, the role of the laity in this kind of calling is crucial to the effectiveness of a visitation evangelism program.

Laypersons have problems in the amount of time they can give in preparation and visitation. Most laypersons work during the daytime, and their evenings are frequently subscribed to other commitments. When the importance of calling is placed before laypeople, many respond. Note that not all laypersons make good callers, anymore than all laypersons make good teachers. Therefore, a very select group of persons should be asked to call. It takes the kind of individual who is sound psychologically and is not threatened by someone's anger or other strong feelings.

There are training procedures that can be used for local laypersons, particularly if the pastor is not skilled in the visitation process. A two to three hour workshop, a one day seminar, or a weekend retreat can provide effective settings for laypersons to learn visitation skills.

As members of the congregation attempt to keep a balance in relationship to the church's activities and remain active participants, it is important to note when these persons begin to become upset over church related conflicts. This is observed in personal conflicts with the pastor or lay members. Signals of stress, anger, and anxiety are noted when financial, social, and moral conflicts are experienced.

Both laity and clergy need to understand the signals, perceive them for what they really are, and deal with them effectively. Almost without exception, the person who has been hurt and angered will give signals, i.e., "I don't know whether I want to keep this job another year," "Church work is becoming boring," "Worship doesn't have as much meaning as it used to have," or "I don't know if I can take all this work anymore." These responses are significant signals and represent. the giving-up stage in a person's relationship to the church. The person may not give up but is in the process of working through some serious feelings and relationships. When these signals are given, the effective layperson, trained in coping with the apathetic and bored parishioner, can learn to short-circuit the falling-out stage. This is done by responding, visiting, phoning, or otherwise supporting those persons who are in a stage of grief and agony in the decision making process of remaining in the active life of the church. These characteristics must be noted in training procedures, as they are indicative of the needs of other human beings.

Training of laity at district levels can follow the same procedures as those for the pastor. The district can provide training on one night or a weekend, or even a full week retreat if necessary. The district executives of denominations are frequently responsible for programming and can facilitate this kind of training through the structure of that denomination. In many ways it is more feasible to train persons, at least initially, at the district level. Frequently, the denomination has funds that can subsidize this type of training.

Many laypersons are highly involved in ecumenical activities: councils of churches, leagues of churches, and other kinds of interdenominational endeavors. It is through these kinds of structures that training can be provided at the immediate level beyond the local church.

Visiting the Apathetic and Bored Church Member

The import of this chapter makes sense only when the pastor or layperson enters the home to make a call. Thus, it is important for the caller to have a grasp of data and background information provided in this work.

Like medication, instruction can be given when none is needed. It is also possible, as in prescribing medication, to instruct when some other remedy would be more appropriate. Instruction and practical experience are both necessary for training the pastor and layperson. It is as important for the pastor or layperson to know how to make a diagnostic evaluation of the person on whom they have called as it is for a physician to make a diagnosis before prescribing medication or surgery. If training is going to take place, the caller must make the connection between the problem and solution, between the need for instruction and the nature of the instruction. Wherever instruction exists, one should be able to see the connection between that instruction and the reason of its existence. [2] The caller should be clear why the call is being made and what he or she needs to do on an inactive member for reasons of securing background and feelings, it is necessary to discuss the implications and procedures of the initial interview.

There are two levels of the interview. One is an ostensible level where observations are made on surface behavior, easily perceived and recorded. The second dimension is to note the unintentional meaning between words. These are messages seen in the person's body language and the sequence of events described. The second level requires considerable training and experience.

The major purpose of this call is to diagnose the difficulty and bring about change in behavior and feelings. There are four kinds of behaviors that can follow a program working with inactive members. The persons can remain inactive and do nothing about the position which they are in. They can return to a moderately active position, less than the original position, but more active than the present position. They can return to an active level of participation. The fourth alternative is to move away from that local congregation and join another church. The direction of that movement will depend on the needs and responses of the interviewee. Let me now return to some of the interviewing procedures.

The interview is open-ended, following the lead of the parishioner, but with the knowledge that certain kinds of information are needed. One important fundamental: the caller has not come to judge or condemn. This does not need to be verbalized, but the behavior and attitude of the interviewer should make this position clear. To be an excellent listener is of first importance. To broaden the listening concepts mentioned above, I would like to describe five components that contribute to effective interpersonal communications. These can be helpful to the pastor or layperson who is in the midst of the interview.

(1) *Self-concept.* An important single factor effecting persons' communications with others is their self-concept; that is, the way they see themselves and their situations. Many times situations change rapidly, but people's beliefs about themselves are always determining factors in their communicative behavior. In one sense of the word, the self is the star in every act of communication. The person who leaves the active life of the church is undergoing a major new self-concept; one that is now distant from the institutional church. This brings feelings with much emotional loading. Many of the hopeless-bored persons reflect poor self-images and see themselves with feelings that are unworthy, inadequate, and inferior. They express lack of confidence and think that their ideas are uninteresting to others and not worth communicating. Because these persons do not see themselves as having much worth, they may become seclusive and guarded in their communications, and particularly neglecting their own ideas. Concepts of the self are not only important for the callee but also for the caller, since there will be transference and counter-transference reaction (to be discussed later) in the interview.

(2) *Listening.* Reik[3] speaks about a process of effective listening called "listening with the third ear." He talks about listening for meanings behind words. He claims that a listener's third ear hears what is said between sentences and without words. He also hears soundless expressions which the speaker feels and thinks. As I have pointed out before, the listener does not sit passively, nodding his head like those little animals that sit in the back of car windows, but the effective listener interacts with the speaker in developing meaning and reaching a common understanding. The following list, taken from Reik's work, will help to clarify and expand previous notions regarding the active listening process:

1. The listener should have a reason or purpose for listening.

2. It is important for the listener to suspend judgment initially.

3. The listener should resist distractions, noises, views, people, and focus only on the speaker.

4. The listener should wait before responding to the speaker. Too prompt a response reduces listening effectiveness.

5. The listener should repeat verbatim what the speaker says.

6. The listener should rephrase in his own words the content and feeling of what the speaker says, to the speaker's satisfaction.

7. The listener should seek the important themes of what the speaker says by listening through the words for the real meaning.

8. The listener should use the time differential between the rate of speech (100-150 words per minute) and the rate of thought (400-500 words per minute)

to reflect upon content and to search for meaning.

9. The listener should be ready to respond to the speaker's comments.

(3) *Clarity of expression.* As effective listening is often neglected in communications, so many find it difficult to say what they mean or express how they feel. Often they assume that other persons understand what they mean, even if what they are saying is ambiguous and uncertain. In many ways they seem to think that people should be able to read the other's minds. "If it is clear to me, it must also be clear to you." This rather startling assumption is one of the most difficult barriers to break down in successful human communication. Part of the purpose of the interview will be to clarify the feelings, attitudes, and knowledge that the person is expressing about his or her particular problem. In the interview, the interviewer will touch sensitive areas in the life of the parishioner. This may cause anxiety, and the person will immediately change the subject or will deliberately make statements to cause confusion and distract the interviewer. The interviewer needs to be observant of these changes in subject matter because they become warnings of sensitive feelings. These feelings can later be brought into the conversation and tenderly probed. The more the interviewer can help the parishioner clarify his or her feelings, the greater the amount of communication can take place. This leads to the fourth communicative procedure—coping with angry feelings.

(4) *Coping with angry feelings.* It was noted in Chapter 4 that anger is a major concern in moving away from a parish. In many of the interviews I conducted, anger became a major concern on the part of the parishioner, and I personally experienced a number of persons break down in tears during the interview. Some became boisterous and even hostile, therefore expressing considerable anger at the institutional church, the pastor, or other persons in the life of the church.

The interviewer will have to cope with his or her own feelings about the anger of the parishioner, particularly when a pastor is hearing condemnation or debasement by one of his or her own parishioners. At that point, it is important to help the parishioner understand his or her anger and also become aware of the anger within one's self.

Some guidelines helpful in talking with an angry member are: Try to be aware of your own emotions as much as possible. Be willing to admit your emotions; do not ignore them or deny them. Try to *own* your own emotions, and be willing to accept responsibility for what you do with them. The interviewer must investigate his or her own emotions and not use rebuttal to win an argument. One should help the parishioner find congruent communications, which means an accurate match between what you and the person are saying and experiencing.[4] Part of the ability to deal with one's anger leads us into the fifth and final

83

brief vignette on communication.

(5) *Self-disclosure* is the fifth of the components that lead to effective interpersonal communications. Sidney Jourard states in his books, *The Transparent Self*[5] and *Self-Disclosure*,[6] that self-disclosure is the ability to talk truthfully and fully about one's self. It is a necessary dimension to effective communication. Jourard further says that an individual cannot really communicate with another person, or get to know that person, unless in the midst of that communication there is an engagement in self-disclosure.

A synonym for self-disclosure is revelation. A revelatory dynamic exists in the interviewing process. The interviewer provides and stimulates a situation in which the parishioner can reveal many different aspects about himself or herself, therefore allowing the pastor or layperson to become a help-agent in cooperation with the parishioner. The self-disclosure, or revelation, will only take place when both parties, the interviewer and the parishioner, trust each other. If a parishioner refuses to share, there is no way for communication to take place. It is the disclosure of self in these interviews that is both painful and healing. Many of the interviewees shared that talking about their feelings was very helpful. Several persons said that no one had ever listened to their story. They thanked me for allowing them this opportunity.

This revelatory process requires a considerable amount of trust. It has been show statistically (see Chapter 3) that a good interviewer can set the apathetic and bored person at ease. Trust begets trust, and self-disclosure generates self-disclosure. The effective interviewer, as an effective communicator, is one who can create a climate of trust in which mutual self-disclosure can occur. The interviewer does not expose himself or herself during the *initial* interview, except as it may be appropriate.

We have seen that there are at least five components in communication during an interview. These are: an adequate self-concept, the ability to be a good listener, the skill of expressing one's thoughts and ideas clearly, being able to cope with emotions such as anger in a functional manner, and the willingness to disclose one's self to others.

Because the interviewer is not only trying to communicate but is taking a religious history, certain areas of information need to be explored. There are ostensible data such as family structure, occupation, and age. In exploring the number of churches a person had joined, the interviewer gets insight into the behavior in former churches.

Other behaviors are examined. Does one pledge? Is one serving on any committee? What is one's attitude at worship now? What was it a year ago? What is happening in his or her reference to worship and education? Is there any change in the behavior over a several year period? If so, what does that look like? Is the church member able to

84

articulate his or her Christian faith? Is there any inter-family conflict in reference to the church? What precipitants provided the setting for leaving the active relationship to the church?

The interviewer needs to note what is being said (taking notes during the interview is not recommended), not just the words but the meaning beyond the verbal statements. The interviewer will cover subjects such as living situation, relationship with God, and the use of faith in daily decisions. This information may be sketchy in an hour interview, but sufficient data can be secured to create a plan of action.

Diagnosis. This section will illustrate the diagnostic procedure. I shall consider methods of diagnosing the apathetic, bored, and the undifferentiated.

The helpless person is easily distinguished. Major factors are quite prominent and easily picked up by the interviewer. A major characteristic of the helpless person is one's institutional blame bias. His or her outward blame states that if the elements outside of him or her would change, he or she would respond. Numerous comments on the interview sheets noted that if a given situation or situations would change, people would return. In one case it was changing the educational program; in another it was removing the minister. This person feels helpless about effecting the external situation and bides time in hopes that the problem will change or go away.

The apathetic person is one who has not done anything about his or her problem, except to suppress it for an interim period. Sometimes the suppressing process can be permanent; whereas other times, if the situation changes externally, the person can respond and change his or her behavior. The person's words, feelings, and aggressive behaviors also indicate the helpless state. For the apathetic person there is more external agitation. A pattern of condemning and striking out at groups and individuals is more explicit.

Apathetic persons have a difficult time getting in touch with their own feelings and acknowledging that they are angry. In several of the interviews individuals were not able to "own" their anger, but always referred to "they." These individuals found it difficult to use the word "I," therefore owning their own anger and taking responsibility for it.

The apathetic group was waiting for changes to take place in the life of the church so they could return. Their phrases, "That is my church," and "I'm just waiting until things change so that I can return," are typical. One other characteristic of apathetic oriented persons is that when things go right in their lives, they will also be complimentary about that. In one of the interviews it was reported that an individual and his wife went to a church after moving to their new community and felt that the church was cold, that persons did not pay any attention to them, and they did not seem welcome. After attending that church for two

Sundays, they went to one of the four churches in the study. There they were received warmly, welcomed with a great deal of personal attention, and were stimulated by the congregation. They joined that church. This information was noted in the first five minutes of the interview, and the interviewer perceived that these characteristics would tend to lead the persons into apathetic behaviors. They became one of our classic cases in the apathetic category, as they were 100 percent externally blame oriented. They were not able to own the feelings of anger and disappointment. The above characteristics are those which the interviewer will need to note when trying to decide if an individual is on the apathetic track.

Let us now turn to the bored parishioner and some of the characteristics signaling this kind of behavior and affect. In contrast to the helpless-apathetic person, the hopeless-bored person will turn most of the anger upon himself or herself. He or she will not be externally blame bias, but self blame bias, and will accept upon his or her own shoulders the blame for that which took place in the church. The phrases, "It's my fault," "I wasn't worthy to do that," "It's not that the minister gives poor sermons, I just don't have the ability to understand them," are actual phrases taken from the interview sheets and are typical responses. These persons exhibit feelings of low self-worth; they tend to be depressed and are frequently withdrawn into themselves. They exhibit a considerable amount of guilt and shame over leaving the church and are very easily hurt by other parishioners who tend to push them to return. The hopeless person will be more apologetic and will frequently make statements asking for forgiveness. This is in contrast to the helpless-apathetic person, who will not confess that he or she did anything wrong but wants the institution to say it was in error.

The distinction between the bored and apathetic parishioner is easily distinguishable, and it should not be too confusing for the interviewer to clarify the two dimensions. Arthur Schmale claims that a person cannot be both apathetic and bored simultaneously; they will either exhibit the traits of one or the other. This leads me to the final and most difficult diagnosis, that of the "undifferentiated" person.

In the research project we found that the persons who were most difficult to diagnose were in the A category. These were persons who were very active and did not exhibit, to any extreme degree, the apathetic or bored concepts. However, those persons interviewed in the B and C categories were easily diagnosed as apathetic or bored. If, in the interview, you discover a person who does not exhibit either characteristic strongly, but tends to move from one to the other in a moderate way, you will need to explore other dimensions of the person's life. There might be family problems, financial problems, theological issues, or other more subtle difficulties. In my experience the person in the undifferentiated state will not be in the disinterested categories. These persons are able to resolve their conflicts and not move to apathetic or bored positions.

Next I shall discuss the plan of action when working with the apathetic or bored person.

The action plan. This section will, by necessity, be incomplete because there has not been sufficient data or research to back up what is suggested. Let me briefly share some concepts of action for the apathetic member.

If the diagnosis has determined the parishioner is apathetic, several steps can be taken. The first response is to make the parishioner aware that persons in the church care about what is happening to him or her. To get at the root of the apathetic member's problem (unresolved anxiety), the caller must deal with the person's perceptions of himself or herself. If a layperson or the pastor takes the time to engage this person with caring concern, I believe this is more helpful than any other kind of program that the local church could provide.

In many ways these persons feel isolated from the community; they feel shut-off and hurt. The re-establishing of communications with them, caring for them with a patient listening ear, and stimulating them with some kind of work they can give to the church, can bring significant results. I have found this to be true by working with many of these persons in my own parish. As mentioned before, it will take a considerable amount of research and follow-through in the years to come to back this up with any specific statistics.

The final section of this chapter is devoted to the bored parishioner. I discussed the nature of the bored person with Dr. Schmale of the School of Medicine, University of Rochester. He affirmed my own personal experience that the bored person is one of the most difficult persons with whom to work. He states that it is important to find the "red line" which ties this person's life together. He also claims that it is difficult to find the "red line" as it takes a considerable amount of personal time and work. Because bored persons are persons who do not have positive self images and are self blame oriented, it is very easy to make them feel guiltier and drive them further away from the church.

The church tends to use guilt as a manipulative device. Bored members will rebel at this and will turn away from that church which uses guilt feelings as a weapon. Telling them that they are sinners, that God will punish them if they do not return to the active life of the church, will do an insurmountable amount of damage and can almost guarantee an inactive relationship. These persons can be helped, however, in groups where there can be a considerable amount of confirmation and affirmation. I believe that this is one of the key responses the church can make to these kinds of persons. They also need to be given jobs and responsibilities in alignment with their abilities. In many ways these persons come through as childlike with statements such as, "I can't do that," "I don't know how to do that," "I'm not good enough to do that," "I don't have the skill to do that." Though in some cases these may be realistic terms, frequently the feelings of these persons are totally irrational.

The bored member will tend to feel sorry and even sad when sharing his or her story. Empathy and identification with his or her feelings are important. Another procedure in helping the bored person is having a caring, sensitive, and patient layperson work with him or her to develop a friendship and support system which can help to affirm the person's worth.

It is very easy to get into a hassle and endless argument with this person. It starts out very simply and within two or three exchanges of conversation the interviewer can be in a bind. The following is a brief example:

Pastor: Mrs. Jones, I remember when you were treasurer and did such an excellent job in the capacity.

Parishioner: Pastor, I didn't feel I was nearly good enough, nor did I have enough training for that job. I felt I really did a very poor job.

Pastor: But, Mrs. Jones, I remember all the good comments that were made about you when you were treasurer.

Parishioner: No, I gave up the job because I was not able to do it well enough, and I got very discouraged.

Pastor: Gee, Mrs. Jones, I thought you really did a good job.

Parishioner: No, Pastor, I really didn't do a good job. I did a bad job.

The two are now locked into an impossible situation, where the pastor is telling Mrs. Jones that she is ok, but Mrs. Jones is telling the pastor she is not ok. This is a typical response and the kind of cyclical difficulty that can develop. It is necessary for the pastor or layperson to get the parishioner stating those things that he or she feels he or she has done well. Almost every person has done something well in his or her life. Only the extremely deprived person would fall into a category where one feels so insufficient and inferior to everyone else that one cannot name some good things that have been accomplished. These good elements are the "red line" to this person's life. To get the person to affirm one's self and follow up on that affirmation is to begin to help the process of letting this person know his or her own worth.

Regardless of whether one is dealing with apathetic or bored persons, it will inevitably be necessary to help these individuals retrace the events which cause them to leave the church. This means there will be a considerable amount of anger, either turned outward upon the caller, or in upon themselves. Only after retracing the tracks of their behavior will persons be able to recover some of their feelings and effectively deal with them. Whether these procedures are done through group processes, institutional programs, or through a caring pastor or layperson is the decision of the local church. One attempt to do this in my own congregation is to establish what we call a "Clinker in Your Thinker" seminar, in which persons come with particular kinds of problems, regardless of what the problems are. Similar kinds of programs, plus a variety of others that the reader might create, could be effective devices in helping these persons re-establish their life in the church.

It may be that the individuals will choose to leave that church altogether. This action may be a healthy move because it indicates disengaging and re-engaging in persons' lives. The purpose is to move persons from their apathetic or bored states to active members of a congregation for the sake of Jesus Christ. It may not be the congregation of which they are now a member, nor even a new congregation, but another institution which is church based.

CONCLUSION

This chapter has systematically explored some of the characteristics of training clergy and laity in visitation procedures. I have dealt with training methodologies including team building, listening skills, and practice calls. I have discussed training in particular terms of the clergy at the local, district, regional, and national levels. I have considered the training of laity and their particular and important role in the visitation program. Laity training was developed at local, district, regional, and national levels. A look at visiting the apathetic and bored church member and dealing with important issues of the initial interview were also considered. I concluded with a brief understanding of some of the action plans that might be applied to help the apathetic and bored church member.

I now move on to the final chapter of this work which will contain a review of all five preceding chapters. It will allow a final evaluation and a brief perspective of this work.

NOTES

[1] Frederic R. Sterns, *Anger: Psychology, Physiology, Pathology* (Springfield: Charles C. Thomas, 1972), p. 56.

[2] Robert F. Mager, *Goal Analysis* (Belmont: Lear, Siegler, Inc./Feoron Publishers, 1972), pp. 4-5.

[3] T. Reik, *Listening with the Third Ear* (New York: Pyramid Publications, 1972).

[4] Myron R. Chartier, "Five Components Contributing to Effective Interpersonal Communications," *The 1974 Annual Handbook for Group Facilators*, eds. J. William Pfeiffer, John E. Jones (La Jolla: Unversity Associates Publishers, Inc., 1974), p. 127.

[5] Sidney Jourard, *Self-disclosure* (New York: Wiley Interscience, 1971).

[6] Sidney Jourard, *The Transparent Self*, (Rev. ed.) (New York: Van Norstrand Reinhold, 1971).

Chapter 6

Summary

This chapter contains descriptions of the presenting problem, research methodology, findings, and conclusions drawn as a result of those findings. It will allow the reader a brief glimpse at the major issues resulting from the data in the preceding five chapters.

A BRIEF DESCRIPTION OF THE PRESENTING PROBLEM

This research project is a result of my awareness that a large number of persons in my parish were once very active but over a period of two or three years became completely inactive and disinterested, yet remained on the church rolls. These persons caused me to raise the following questions. What are the psychological and theological dynamics which occur in the life of a church member who is at one time active and two or three years later is inactive? Where do the affects of apathy and boredom originate? What are the behavioral differentiations that take place as a result of anxiety producing events? Does the inactive church member feel helpless or hopeless? Are there some precipitants which occur more frequently than others? Do members leaving the church blame themselves, or is there outward blame toward the institutional church? How can this differentiation be determined?

The power and strength of the local congregation is only as stable as those who make up its membership. When a congregation loses persons who have contributed much time and energy, it loses a percentage of its ability to be an effective witness for Christ in the world. To find a way of effectively slowing or stopping the rate of attrition would be beneficial both to the strength of the local church and to the individuals who may potentially be lost to the community of faith.

There are two major questions which are answered in this book: Why do persons leave who are active? What can be done about it? Only the first question was studied in this research. The second question is answered hypothetically, and until research can be completed on the suggested methods in Chapter 5, many questions will have to go unanswered.

THE RESEARCH METHODOLOGY

This research project was conducted in four United Methodist Churches of the Western New York Conference: Christ View, Henrietta; Fairport; Orchard Park; and Epworth, Jamestown. All four churches had memberships of 400-800 and were located in suburban type communities. All churches had the same clergypersons for at least four years and had persons who fell into the categories of active, less active, and inactive relationships.

Each church provided names of fifteen or more families in each of three activity levels. Group A is persons who have been active in the church for at least three years, have made a pledge to the church program, have served on one or more committees for at least a three year period, and have attended worship seventy-five percent or more of the time.

Group B is persons who were at one time in the A category but are now moving into a less active relationship. These are persons who are not serving on any committee or are serving in a minimal way. They have decreased their attendance at worship by at least twenty-five percent or more, have lowered their pledges, and expressed less emotional support of the church program and mission.

Group C became the inactive individuals in the study. They were in the A group, then moved to the B group, and now are completely inactive. These persons do not serve on any committees, do not pledge to the financial support of the church, and do not attend worship, except on very special occasions. They show very little or no response to the needs of the church and have become distant and disinterested.

When the names of the families were secured, a letter was sent to them asking their participation in the research project. Letters were sent to 236 members in the four churches. Each letter had a return card to indicate a desire to take part in the research by having a home interview. A total of 101 persons responded, and these persons were divided into the three groups: 61—active, 17—less active, and 23—inactive.

Twenty clergypersons were trained in a one day event to conduct interviews in 60 homes located in the four parishes. After some dropout of the interviewers, 13 persons interviewed the 101 persons.

The interview was held with the adults of the family; youth and children were not included in the survey. Ninety-five percent of the interviews were held with married couples, the other five percent being singles, widows, widowers, etc.

There were no forms filled out by the interviewers. All of the information was gathered through an open-ended interview, where not only specific data were secured but feelings and attitudes were explored. After the interview was over, the interviewer filled in the data sheets and returned them to me for compilation. The data sheets and check lists were divided into six major sections: (1) fixed data: income, age, sex, etc.; (2) behavior: worship attendance, pledging, etc.; (3) precipitants: items causing anxiety or anger, i.e., conflict with pastor, other church members, family members, theological issues, etc.; (4) situation: living situation (with or without mate and/or children), employment, etc.; (5) religious status: an attempt was made to find if persons see God as an active agent in the world, whether these persons use their faith to make decisions, and how they use the Bible in their lives; (6) how they became involved in churches they had joined, how they left the churches (list of incidents that occurred), suggested follow-ups that would be needed to help these persons, and finally, a description of the helpless-hopeless characteristics of the persons interviewed.

Upon receiving all of the data sheets from the 13 interviewers, statistical analysis was completed and projections made. The Chi-square test was used to check the resulting random probabilities. The significance level of .05 was established.

THE FINDINGS

The purpose of the statistical work was to find relationships between the active, less active, and inactive members of the church; were they different than each other? If so, how?

Certain categories proved to be significantly different in the activity groups. The A group was used as the norm. When there is variance, it is away from that active behavior. There are four types of distinctions made in this analysis: the significant differences between the A and B groups, the A and C groups, a classification of the A group and those areas which were significant for both B and C groups, and a final comparison between the B and C groups without reference to the active members (A).

The following areas were found to be significantly different between the active (A) and less active (B) church members. The less active members are described as being older than the A group, serve less on committees, worship less frequently, have a higher frequency of change in worship habits, have difficulty articulating their faith, express conflict with other members of their own family, feel overworked in the church, have conflict over educational issues, and are involved more in community activities than are the active members. They do not see God as active in the world, are less prone to speak of Christ as Lord, and are not familiar with church structure. Less active members do not use their faith as frequently to make decisions. They are not recipients of the church's services as often as active members. Less active members also hold the Bible as a less important book in their lives. These areas are significant at the .05 level of significance.

The above items illustrate those components which begin to change in the dropout pattern. Behaviors, feelings, attitudes, etc. begin to take on certain characteristics between active and less active members.

When comparing active church members with inactive members, there are slightly different patterns.

Inactive members exhibit the following characteristics when compared with active church members. Disinterested (apathetic or bored) members give less financially, do not serve on committees, attend worship less frequently, have a higher frequency of change in worship habits, are not able to articulate their faith as clearly (if at all), have considerably more conflict with the pastor, other church members, and their own families. Inactive members have more conflict over financial issues and express feelings of being overworked in the church. They do not speak of Christ as Lord as frequently, are not as familiar with church structure, and do not see themselves as recipients of the church's services. They also hold the Bible as a less important book.

Those areas in which both the B and C groups are different than active members fall into somewhat of a different pattern than any of the singular categories mentioned above. Both less active and inactive members serve less on committees, worship less frequently, do not articulate their faith as clearly, have more conflict with their family members over church issues, feel overworked, express conflict over educational matters, and speak less frequently of Christ as Lord. The less active and inactive members also are less familiar with church structure, and see themselves as recipients of the church's services less frequently than active members. Finally, both less active and inactive members see the Bible as a less important book in their lives than the active members of a local church.

The fourth comparison clarified relationships between the B and C groups without reference to the active members. Special attention is given to several characteristics. There is a distinctive shift in articulating one's faith between the B and C groups. When a person is moving away from active participation, one's religious language is suppressed. When the individual has dropped out, the member is able to recover some of the lost religious language. A similar pattern occurs in other religious ideations such as seeing God active in the world, speaking of Christ as Lord, and using faith to help make decisions. In each case the Bs show lower responses than the Cs, which indicates the Cs recapture some of the original behaviors they exhibited as As.

The following categories of study did not prove significantly different between active (A) and less active (B) members. Both groups gave the same financially. They did not change their frequency of worship and had the same level of conflict with the pastor (very low level). Their family incomes, occupational spread, and education did not prove to be significantly different. Like active members, less active persons did not church hop and showed relatively low anxiety levels during the interviews. They both had little or no conflict with other church members and showed no differences in conflictual matters regarding theology. They recorded the same responses when talking about financial issues in the church. There were no differences in seeing God as inside or outside of themselves, and they saw themselves in the same way regarding the self-image of being a minister to others (a very positive image).

The research results in this work pointed out several areas that remained the same between active (A) and inactive members (C). The following list is composed of those items which did not prove to be significantly different: age, family income, occupation, education levels, church hopping, anxiety during the interviews, theological issues, education issues, involvement in the community, God as an active agent in the world, God as seen outside or inside of self, using faith to make decisions, and sees self as a minister to others. My study indicates there is no statistical difference in the above items between active church members and disinterested members.

Several other important items came to light in the study. One major function of the research was to note the differences in feelings regarding anxiety, anger, helplessness, and hopelessness. When comparing existing literature with the feelings shared by these 101 persons, certain patterns began to become very evident.

Both less active and inactive church members showed considerably less ability to cope with conflictual situations. All persons, with the exception of one person in the inactive category, could relate to a given event which made them anxious and which started them moving away from their active church relationships. When the anxiety reached a certain level (beyond toleration), they became angry, changed their relationships with the congregation, and moved into an inactive relationship.

The feeling of anger divides the group into two directions of blame. The apathetic person blames persons (institutions) outside of himself or herself. The tracking away from the active relationship follows predictable patterns once the tracking has begun, providing there is no intervention on the part of members of the church to change the dropout pattern. (In all 23 cases of persons in the inactive category, no member was approached by the pastor or another church member to see why they had left.)

After each interview was completed, the interviewer was asked to briefly describe the orientation toward being helpless (apathetic) or hopeless (bored). These reactions were then compared with the activity level (A, B, C groups). There was clear evidence that there is a distinct shift in the helpless-hopeless orientation as the individuals move further and further from the center of church activity. Active church members have sixty percent of their population with no evidence of being either helpless or hopeless. Thirteen percent exhibited feelings of helplessness; ten percent expressed feelings of hopelessness, while only four percent exhibited both helpless and hopeless feelings. The remaining thirteen percent was not recorded by the interviewers.

When we look at the results of persons who are in the process of moving away from the church (B group), there is a different pattern of response. Only nineteen percent of the less active persons showed integration of their feelings, while fifty percent felt helpless and thirty-one percent hopeless. No one exhibited feelings of both helplessness and hopelessness.

In the inactive group the tracks of apathy and boredom reach their conclusion. No one in the inactive group integrated the two feelings. To the contrary, sixty-six percent of the group displayed very strong and distinctive feelings of helplessness. These became the apathetic population of the inactive group. On the other hand, thirty-three percent of the group fell in the hopeless category and ended as bored church members. This means there were twice as many persons in the group that tended to be outward blame oriented.

These figures show that the further down the dropout track a person travels, the orientation of blame and the intensity of the difficulty becomes clearer. There are very clear differences between the active group and the less active and inactive groups. The long term active church member is one who is able to cope with and integrate the feelings of anxiety, anger, helplessness, and hopelessness. The active church member is one who can use his or her anxiety and anger in a way which does not drive him or her from relations with other active church members.

As a result of the above information, it is possible to track the behavior of a person from an active to inactive status. In the concluding section of this summary, I shall follow the tracks from the beginning in an anxiety situation (conflict with pastor, family member, church member, overworked, etc.) to the point of the giving up (apathy or boredom). I shall also note the giving up stages (hopelessness or help-lessness) as the tracks develop.

CONCLUSIONS

The following description of the dropout tracks is an attempt to pull together all that was found in the original research which I completed with the help of thirteen interviewers, plus the discussion (Chapter 2) of other research materials which related to my thesis. I describe it simply as the delineation of the dropout tracks of the apathetic and bored church member.

The tracking process always begins with anxiety provoking events. The events are usually triggered by personal relationships, i.e., the pastor, other church members, or family members. These events may be perceived as being reality, neurotic, existential, or morally oriented.

When anxiety levels become too much to tolerate, active church members will send out verbal signals for others to hear (the cry for help). If there is no response to these signals, there will tend to be more agitated signals in the form of anger. Persons who express anger at others, including the institution, will follow the apathetic track, while others who express feelings of inward blame and guilt will start down the boredom track. As long as there is a chance for resolution of their anxiety and anger, persons will remain within the active life of the church. When, however, there is no resolution and the anxiety-anger levels become too great to tolerate, active church members will begin to change behavior patterns. This is first noted in their attendance at worship, committee meetings, and dropout of religious language. These behaviors act as additional clues given to the community with hope that someone will take notice that they are extracting themselves from the church. During this time of moving away, persons experience the grief of giving up favorite loved persons and objects. They experience the giving-up complex and suffer from a sense of loss and self-gratification. Unless someone comes to their aid and listens to what is happening to them, they will continue down the track to the complete dropout level.

After a decision to drop out has been made (not always a conscious decision), they will wait six to eight weeks before re-engaging the time usually spent in church activities. This period of "limbo" serves two functions. It allows persons to get in control of the loss they have suffered, and it allows an opportunity to see if anyone from the church will come and talk to them. If no one from the church pays attention to their needs, they will re-engage the hours and energy in other pursuits. About fifty percent of the inactive members will find other activities in the community to which they may give themselves. The other half of the members will drop from all outside activities and devote themselves to their families, homes, sports, etc.

When re-engaging has been completed, persons have reached the bottom of one of the two tracks. If in beginning to drop out they tended to blame themselves for what was going on in their lives, they followed the boredom track. If, on the other hand, they oriented their blame on the outside world of persons and institutions, they followed the apathy track.

Once the bottom of the track has been reached, there is a stabilization process which occurs. They have sufficiently removed themselves from the anxiety setting, but they suffer a sense of loss and frustration which remains indefinitely. Several persons were inactive for ten years and exhibited the same reactions as those who were inactive for shorter periods of time. It is hypothesized, but not researched (see Chapter 5), that these persons will remain inactive until someone from the church meets their needs and listens to their aches and pains.

It is clear from this research that the church of Jesus Christ, if it is going to be an effective instrument to its own membership, needs to sensitize itself to what is going on in the life of its membership. Until that occurs, there will be many persons who will leave the active ranks of our local churches.

Appendix

TABLE 1
Family Units Responding Positively to Letters Sent, and Separated According to Activity Level

Church	Total Sent	As Rec'd	%	Activity Category Bs Rec'd	%	Cs Rec'd	%	Total Rec'd	%
C.V.	79	24 (36)	66.6	8 (20)	40.0	4 (23)	17.4	36	45.6
Fpt	51	13 (21)	61.9	1 (15)	6.6	4 (15)	26.6	18	35.3
O. P.	59	6 (25)	24.0	0 (15)	0.0	1 (19)	5.2	7	11.8
Epwth	47	4 (17)	23.5	1 (15)	6.6	0 (15)	0.0	5	10.6
Total	**236**	**47 (99)**	**47.4**	**10 (65)**	**15.3**	**9 (72)**	**12.5**	**66**	**27.9**

Numbers in ( ) represent the number of letters sent to that category.
The numbers without brackets are the numbers returned.

100

TABLE 2

Total Interviews Completed in all Categories

Church	Category A	B	C	% of Total Calls	Total Interviews
Christ View	41	11	10	60.4	61
Fairport	12	3	11	25.7	26
Orchard Park	6	2	2	9.9	10
Epworth	2	1	0	3.0	3
Total	**61**	**17**	**23**	**99.0**	**101**

TABLE 3

Age Distribution for the A, B, C Groupings

Age	A%	B%	C%	Average % of the Total
20-29	8	0	13	8
30-39	43	11	39	37
40-49	34	52	22	35
50-59	11	18	0	15
60-Up	3	18	0	5

Relationship of A and B significant at the .025 level
Relationship of A and C — No significance*
*No significance = greater than .05

TABLE 4

Financial Distribution According to Activity Groups

Income Group	A%	B%	C%	Total %*
Under $5,000	3	9	0	3
$5,000-9,999	11	9	0	8
$10,000-14,999	17	18	46	23
$15,000-19,999	36	18	23	30
$20,000-29,999	25	27	23	25
$30,000-Up	3	18	7	6
No Answer	5	0	0	3

Relationship of A and B — No significance

Relationship of A and C — No significance

*These totals are based on the number of family units of income, including both husband and wife if they both were employed. There were a total of 60 family units in the study.

TABLE 5

Occupations of the A, B, C Categories

Occupation	A %	B %	C %	Total %
Clerical and related workers	10.6	25.0	14.3	13.7
Craftsmen, foremen, related workers	4.3	8.3	21.4	8.2
Farmers, farm managers	0	0	0	0
Farm laborers and farm foremen	0	0	0	0
Laborers	2.1	8.3	0	2.7
Operatives and related workers	4.3	0	0	2.7
Pivate household workers	0	0	0	0
Professional, technical, related workers	63.8	41.7	57.1	58.9
Proprietors, managers, officials	4.3	8.3	0	4.1
Sales workers	10.6	8.3	7.1	9.6
Totals	**100.0**	**99.9**	**99.9**	**99.9**

Relationship of A and B — No significance

Relationship of A and C — No significance

TABLE 6

Educational Level of the A, B, C Categories

Education Level	A %	B %	C %	Average %
Under 12th grade	1.7	6.3	0	2.0
High school graduate	20.3	18.8	30.4	22.4
1-3 years of college	32.2	31.2	30.4	31.7
4 years of college	27.1	25.0	21.7	25.5
1-4 years graduate school	18.6	18.8	17.3	18.3
Total	**99.9**	**100.1**	**99.8**	**99.9**

Relationship of A and B — No significance

Relationship of A and C — No significance

TABLE 7

Anxiety Level Seen by the Interviewer for the A, B, C Groups

Anxiety Level	A %	B %	C %
Low anxiety (1-3)	77.8	70.6	73.9
Medium anxiety (4-6)	18.5	11.8	17.4
High anxiety (7-10)	3.7	17.6	8.7

Relationship of A and B — No significance

Relationship of A and C — No significance

TABLE 8

Financial Giving Response in the A, B, C Groupings

Giving Response	A %	B %	C %
No pledge given	3.8	7.1	76.9
Pledges given	96.2	92.9	23.1

Relationship of A and B — No significance

Relationship of A and C significant at the .001 level

TABLE 9

Percentage of Persons Serving on One or More Committees

Service Response	A	B	C
Serves on one or more committees	95.1	23.5	0
Serves on no committees	4.9	76.4	100.0

Relationship of A and B significant at the .001 level

Relationship of A and C significant at the .001 level

TABLE 10

Worship Attendance According to Activity Level

Attendance Level		A %	B %	C %
Attendance	0-25%	0	52.9	100.0
	25-50%	11.9	17.6	0
	50-75%	10.2	17.6	0
	75-Up%	77.9	11.8	0

Relationship of A and B significant at the .001 level

Relationship of A and C significant at the .001 level

TABLE 11

Change in Worship Frequency for the A, B, C Groups

Change in Frequency	A %	B %	C %
Stayed same	82.0	76.5	73.9
Went up	11.5	0	0
Went down	6.5	23.5	26.1

Relationship of A and B significant at the .10 level

Relationship of A and C significant at the .05 level

TABLE 12

Ability to Articulate the Christian Faith in the A, B, C Groups

Articulation Level	A %	B %	C %
No articulation	0	47.1	21.7
Moderate	66.1	47.1	52.2
Excellent	33.9	5.8	23.1

Relationship of A and B significant at the .001 level

Relationship of A and C significant at the .001 level

TABLE 13

Conflict with the Pastor as Perceived by the A, B, C Groups

Degree of Conflict	A %	B %	C %
No conflict	77.0	68.8	45.5
Moderate	18.8	31.2	9.0
High	4.2	0	45.5

Relationship of A and B — No significance

Relationship of A and C significant at the .001 level

TABLE 14

Conflict with Another Church Member

Degree of Conflict	A %	B %	C %
No conflict	73.0	57.0	54.0
Moderate	21.0	35.0	14.0
High	6.0	7.0	32.0

Relationship of A and B — No significance

Realtionship of A and C significant at the .025 level

TABLE 15

Conflict with Family Member

Degree of Conflict	A %	B %	C %
No conflict	90.0	41.0	63.0
Moderate	5.0	28.0	11.0
High	5.0	21.0	26.0

Relationship of A and B significant at the .005 level

Relationship of A and C significant at the .025 level

TABLE 16

Conflict with Theological Issues

Degree of Conflict	A %	B %	C %
No conflict	81	70	75
Moderate	18	10	20
High	0	20	5

Relationship of A and B — No significance

Relationship of A and C — No significance

TABLE 17

Conflict over Financial Issues

Degree of Conflict	A %	B %	C %
No conflict	98	100	70
Moderate	2	0	10
High	0	0	20

Relationship of A and B — No significance

Relationship of A and C significant at the .001 level

TABLE 18

Conflict over Educational Issues

Degree of Conflict	A %	B %	C %
No conflict	86	43	74
Moderate	10	29	16
High	4	29	10

Relationship of A and B significant at the.025 level

Relationship of A and C — No significance

TABLE 19

Overworked in Church Activities

Degree of Conflict	A %	B %	C %
No conflict	82	55	53
Moderate	16	9	29
High	2	36	18

Relationship of A and B significant at the .005 level

Relationship of A and C significant at the .05 level

TABLE 20

Involvement in other Community Activities

Degree of Involvement	A %	B %	C %
No involvement	36	62	50
Moderate	55	0	32
High	9	38	18

Relationship of A and B significant at the .005 level

Relationship of A and C — No significance

TABLE 21

Responses to the Concept of Seeing God as Active in the World

No activity	A %	B %	C %
No activity	5	26	4
Moderate	47	53	70
High	48	20	26

Relationship of A and B significant at the .005 level

Relationship of A and C — No significance

TABLE 22

Sees God as Outside or Inside of Self

Degree of Intensity	A %	B %	C %
Outside self (1-3)	20	43	34
Balanced between (4-6)	53	36	48
Inside self (7-9)	27	21	17

Relationship of A and B — No significance

Relationship of A and C — No significance

TABLE 23

Speaks of Christ as Lord and Saviour

Degree of Frequency	A %	B %	C %
Not at all	32	88	74
Seldom	52	6	5
Frequently	16	6	17

Relationship of A and B significant at the .001 level

Relationship of A and C significant at the .001 level

TABLE 24

Familiar with Church Structure

Degree of Familiarity	A %	B %	C %
Not at all	2	18	17
Moderate	44	59	43
Great	54	24	39

Relationship of A and B significant at the .05 level

Relationship of A and C significant at the .05 level

TABLE 25

Uses Faith to Help Make Decisions

Frequency of Using Faith	A %	B %	C %
Not at all	8	35	22
Sometimes	61	53	57
Frequently	31	12	21

Relationship of A and B significant at the .005 level

Relationship of A and C — No significance

TABLE 26

Sees Self as a Minister to Serve Others

Frequency of Service	A %	B %	C %
Not at all	5	13	9
Sometimes	55	44	70
Frequently	40	44	22

Relationship of A and B — No significance

Relationship of A and C — No significance

TABLE 27

Sees Self as a Recipient of Church's Services

Degree of Service	A %	B %	C %
Not at all	17	47	57
Sometimes	46	47	35
Frequently	37	4	7

Relationship of A and B significant at the .01 level

Relationship of A and C significant at the .001 level

TABLE 28

Sees Bible as Important Book

Degree of Importance	A %	B %	C %
Not at all	9	59	39
Sometimes	42	12	39
Frequently	48	24	22

Relationship of A and B significant at the .001 level

Relationship of A and C significant at the .005 level

Letter to Pastors

Dear ...

Enclosed you will find materials regarding the research project I talked to you about over the phone. I think you will find the materials adequate in giving you background for any questions you might have. I do wish to summarize for you, however, what I am asking of you.

First, please send to me 15 names (more if possible) in each of three categories:

A. Persons who are active (hold major or minor positions in the church and have done so for at least three years). This means that a new member who was active in another church, but recently moved to your town, could be included along with those persons of continuous activity. They should have pledged in this current year's budget and have paid at least 80% of that pledge to date (this figure may be hard to get except through your financial secretary—use your own judgement). These persons should also be attending at least 75% of the time in your worship services. Finally, the attitudes of this group of people show concern and maximum support of your local church.

B. This group of persons is defined as those who were *once active*, but who are now becoming less active. They may have lowered their pledge, or not pledged at all this year. They may be serving in some small way in the congregation, but it is considerably less than in the past. Their attendance at worship is less frequent than in the past, and there appears to be a shift of feelings about the church. I recognize that this category is difficult to pinpoint, and it is left up to you to make the decisions. In general terms, it means persons moving away in their interest and involvement.

C. The final group of persons is defined as totally inactive persons. They do not attend church (Christmas and Easter excluded). They have not pledged for at least two years. They have not served on any committee in that period of time, and they appear totally disinterested in anything that the church does or has to say. The main criteria for this, however, is that these persons were *once active* (category A) in your church, but now are not. These are the "dead wood" on your records.

All of the categories include the fact that they are members of your congregation. I am asking for only *individual* names, not couples. We are not going to interview couples or families, but only individuals. This will make a big difference in your choice.

I will need names, addresses and telephone numbers. Please divide the groups according to A, B, C. If you use any teenagers please indicate with a (T) after the name, otherwise I will take it for granted that they are 20 or over. Try to select persons across the age spread in each category, if possible. I am trying to find out what happens at given ages as well as other kinds of correlations.

If, after reading the enclosed materials, you still have questions, please call me and I will be glad to answer them, if it is within my power.

Thank you for your help.

Sincerely yours,

John S. Savage

JSS/pb

I NEED YOUR ASSISTANCE
IN A VERY UNUSUAL RESEARCH PROJECT

Skill training in dealing with low interest and non-participating parishioners is the focus of a research project I am developing. The purpose is to train both clergy and lay persons in effective methods of changing the behavior of and resolving issues in these kinds of specific behaviors.

This research will be used as a basic information in new training modalities for a Doctoral Dissertation which I am now writing as a part of my doctoral requirements at Colgate Rochester/Bexley Hall/Crozer Theological Seminary.

WHAT WILL BE EXPECTED OF YOU

1. Return enclosed card immediately if you wish to be involved.
2. Be present at a one-day training program at the Western New York Conference Center on May 8th from 9:00 AM to 4:00 PM.
3. Make 4 to 8 calls on parishioners in some other nearby parish.
4. Learn a special open-ended religious interview process which will be taught and experienced in the training session.
5. Return interview information for correlation and interpretation.

WHAT YOU WILL RECEIVE FOR YOUR INVOLVEMENT

1. Free training which you can use in your own parish.
2. Training methods from which you can train your own lay persons.
3. I am hoping for funding for this project and thus should be able to pay travel and small honorarium for your trouble, but at this point this is not guaranteed.
4. Some fantastic fellowship with guys and gals you love most.
5. Insights into the nature of the angry and apathetic parishioner.
6. A look at a new systems analysis approach to the supportive systems in the church along with what I am calling "drainage systems."

Data Gathering Forms

Information needs from the interview:

Age: ☐15-19 ☐20-29 ☐30-39 ☐40-49 ☐50-59 ☐60-up

Income: ☐under $5,000 ☐$6,000-10,000 ☐$10,000-15,000

☐$15,000-20,000 ☐$20,000-30,000 ☐$30,000-up

Occupation:_____

Education: Circle Grade or year of College you have completed:

1, 2, 3, 4, 5, 6, 7, 8, 9, 10, 11, 12 College: 1, 2, 3, 4

Graduate School: 1, 2, 3, 4

Are you now a student? ☐Yes ☐No ☐Part-time ☐Full-time

Marital Status: Single ☐Married ☐Separated ☐Divorced

☐Widow ☐Widower

Number of children____, ages_____

☐Male ☐Female

Please give a brief history of your religious (church) affiliations.

1. Year you joined a church for the first time_____.

2. List churches you have been a member of since that time:

Church_____ Denomination_____

City_____ Years of Membership_____

Church_____ Denomination_____

City_____ Years of Membership_____

Church_____ Denomination_____

City_____ Years of Membership_____

Church_____ Denomination_____

City_____ Years of Membership_____

(Add others if necessary)

Interview Check List for Religious History

Fill in the following areas which were evident in the interview you just had. Please add any additional comments you discovered which are not covered on this survey sheet.

BEHAVIOR:

Anxious about interview

(No anxiety — 1 2 3 4 5 6 7 8 9 10 — High anxiety)

☐No pledge given for current year

☐Contributes but does not pledge

☐Pledge given for current year

☐Serves on at least one committee

☐Serves on no committee

Worship attendance now (circle one)   0-25   25-50   50-75   75-up

Worship attendance one year ago (circle one)   0-25 25-50 50-75 75-up

Worship meaningful   (no meaning   some meaning   very meaningful)

Has there been any drastic changes in attendance in the past year

☐Yes   ☐No

☐Illness in family which has house-bound or hospitalized during absence

Inter-family conflict related to church   (no conflict   moderate   great)

Ability to articulate Christian Faith

(no articulation   moderate   excellent)

Add other behaviors you feel were important.

PRECIPITANTS:
(Why did they leave when they did? Circle one or more.)

Conflict with pastor   (no conflict   moderate   high)

Conflict with other church member   (no conflict   moderate   high)

Conflict with family member   (no conflict   moderate   high)

Conflict with other than above   (state)

    (no conflict   moderate   high)

Conflict with theological issues   (no conflict   moderate   high)

Conflict over financial issues   (no conflict   moderate   high)

Conflict over educational issues   (no conflict   moderate   high)

Overworked in church activities   (no   moderate   high)

Church work became meaningless   (no meaning   moderate   great)

Became involved in other community activities
    (no involvement   moderate   high)

List activities outside of church and state length of time involved in these activities.

Had personal problems—needed time to think
    (no problems   moderate   difficult)

☐Death in family

☐Divorce

☐Separation with mate

Felt I wasn't needed   (no feeling   moderate   high)

Felt I was misdirected   (no feeling   moderate   high)

Conflict over moral issues   (no conflict   moderate   high)

Add any additional comments:

SITUATION:

☐Living at home with mate and/or children

☐Living alone

☐Employed   ☐Unemployed   ☐Welfare   ☐Unemployment

☐Retired   ☐Widower   ☐Widow

☐Not attending church anywhere

☐Attending church regularly at another congregation

Add other important information:

RELIGIOUS STATUS:

Sees God as active agent in the world   (no   moderate   high)

Sees God as outside of self — 1 2 3 4 5 6 7 8 9 10 — inside one's self
(circle one)

Speaks of Christ as Lord and Saviour   (not at all   seldom   frequently)

Familiar with church structure
(not at all   moderate knowledge   great knowledge)

Uses faith to help make decisions   (not at all   sometimes   frequently)

Sees self as a "minister" to serve others
(not at all   sometimes   frequently)

Sees self as recipient of church's services
(not at all   sometimes   frequently)

Sees Bible as important Book   (not at all   sometimes   frequently)

Describe any other religious ideations:

LIST SEQUENCE OF RELIGIOUS EVENTS:

List in order how they became involved in churches they have joined, particularly the one they are now a member of:

List in order how they left the church. List incidents.

Suggest follow-up needed on this call.
What could you suggest be done to help this person? State:

Describe the helpless-hopeless characteristics of this person.

Below are a list of hypotheses which I bring to the project. The list represents a series of statements which I hope to prove to be true (I may find, of course, that they are all, or in part, false as well). Since I know of no other emperical data to prove them one way or other, I wish to investigate these issues with effective research procedures.

1. There are specific psychodynamic events which occur in the life of an individual that allows him/her to move from being center-core in the church to a totally uninvolved member.
2. Stages which occur in these movements are predictable.
3. Methods can be learned to reverse this process.
4. For the best interest of the church, these patterns need to be reversed.
5. There are dynamic differences between the member who remains active and the one who completely drops out.

6. Unresolved anger, frustration, helplessness and hopelessness are the propellants to uninvolvement.

7. The issues of forgiveness, reconciliation and rejection are theological components which effect this behavior.

8. The meaning of the church as a community of faith to those who are uninvolved is a central issue.

9. Methods of training can be created to train clergy and laity to encounter these issues.

10. A training program is worth the time and money.

11. The church should spend its energy and efforts on developing more skills and knowledge in these issues.

12. The institutional structure has a direct effect upon decisions of persons and their movement.

Letter to Interviewee

I would like to ask your help in an important research project regarding the effectiveness of the Church in our time. This project has been approved by the Western New York Conference of the United Methodist Church and my Dissertation Committee of Colgate Rochester/Bexley Hall/Crozer Theological Seminaries. In order to get your candid opinions, I would very much like to have the privilege of having one of our interviewers talk with you sometime later this spring when this research project will be undertaken. Communities involved in this project are Fairport, Buffalo, Jamestown and Henrietta.

Would you please cooperate in doing this? I believe it will be helpful to all churches, as well as meaningful for you to take part. The interviews will take about 50 minutes and will be conducted by a trained clergy interviewer in your home. The interviewer does not live in your community. All interviews will be anonymous in nature and all information will be handled with professional standards of confidentiality.

Would you check yes on the enclosed card and return it to us today? An appointment secretary will call you at a later date to make arrangements for an interviewer to visit you. The interviews will be held between May 9 and May 22.

The results of this research will be published in a doctoral dissertation which I am writing as a part of my requirements for a Doctor of Ministry Degree at Colgate Rochester/Bexley Hall/Crozer Theological Seminaries.

I thank you for your help in this important project.

Sincerely yours,

John S. Savage

JSS/pb
Enc.

125

MEMO TO: Pastors of Western New York Conference

FROM: John (Tim) Savage

RE: Visitation Evangelism Research Project
           Training — May 8th, 9:00 AM - 4:00 PM

There is not one church in our Conference that does not have on its membership lists, a group of uninvolved, uninterested persons. If you look at your records, the chances are many of your parishioners were once very active, inner-core members, but now they never come to Worship, do not take part in church committees or activities. They will not pledge to the budget and seem to be totally out of it, yet they do not want their membership removed from that local congregation.

I have designed a research project which specifically deals with this problem. I am asking your help in that project. Enclosed you will find an information sheet which I wish you would read, and to which I hope you will respond. You will also find a list of other pastors in our Conference who are invited to participate. The more who will help, the more we will learn, and the more we'll be trained to help others in this vital task.

This research project is approved by the Conference Committee on Planning and Research which endorses its purpose and procedure. If you agree to help, please return the card as soon as possible, and read the additional materials for further details.

Hope to see you.

Response Cards

Pastor

Dear Tim:

☐I would be glad to take part in the training for interviewing persons in the Conference Research Project. I will be present on May 8th at the Conference Center at 9:00 AM.

☐Sorry, I cannot help.

Name _____

Address _____

Phone _____

Interviewee

Dear Mr. Savage:

☐I would be willing to have an interviewer talk with me about the effectiveness of the church in our time.

☐I am unable to help in your Research Project.

Name _____

Address _____

Phone _____

Training for Research Interviews

1. Callers arrive and make name tags.
2. Gather into groups of six.
3. Write on newsprint three or four words of what you feel like when you call on a stranger—on an inactive member—on an angry member.
4. Diagram with some symbol a representative form for each kind of visit.
5. Discuss these feelings with your group of six (three?).
6. Instructions:
   a. The person you call on will be more frightened, anxious, etc. than you. You know what is going to happen; he does not.
   b. You need to be in touch with your own anxiety so that you can be in touch with his.
7. The Research Project
   a. The purpose of the research
      - What I hope to find (p. 8 in paper)
   b. The psychological background
      - The Anxiety-Anger Complex (discuss)
   c. Anger, Boredom, Apathy
      - An understanding
   d. Methodology of the Research Project
      - The sample (how we got it and why)
      - The response (feedback on returned cards)
      - Statistics
      - Johari's window
   e. Calling skills
      - Listening skills
      - Telephone skills
      - Interviewing skills
      - Pick up cards
      - Role-play
      - Fill out form after interview

MATERIALS:	PROCESS:

MATERIALS:

Name tags
Newsprint
Crayons
Envelopes
Stamps
Suggestions for callers
Thesis papers
Anger Complex forms
Paper (plain)
History check lists

PROCESS:

Put up goals for the day

Goals:

1. To train you how to make an effective:
   a. phone call for an appointment
   b. interview
2. To give you understandings of the nature of the bored and apathetic parishioner
3. To instruct you on the administrative procedures of the research

FORM A

My name is _____

My immediate family includes _____

My job in my local church is _____

My occupation is _____

FORM B

What I am proud about in my church is _____

When I call on strangers, I feel _____

The thing I like most about myself is _____

I am happiest when _____

Suggestions for Callers

Before you call: With your partner —

1. Be clear on your purpose in calling.

   Our primary concern is to express our interest in and concern for fellow members of our church as well as constituents and to engage in a dialogue of active listening and sharing of our faith.

2. Review what you know about the family on whom you are calling.

During the call:

1. Introduce yourself and your reason for calling. Clarify why you are calling on this particular family.

2. Engage in active listening:

   Paraphrase to make sure you understand what is said.

   e.g. "You're saying that your real interest is in community service, not church work."

   Check for feelings that are expressed verbally or non-verbally.

   e.g. "You felt left out by the last group you attended?"
   "You felt kind of irritated by some of the things the church does."

   Clarify what is said.

   e.g. "You mean it is your work schedule that keeps you from attending, not your lack of interest."

   Question to draw out feelings and concerns.

   e.g. "What yould would you really like to see the church do?"

   Active listening is most effective when it is non-judgemental, non-defensive, and reflects a genuine desire to hear what the other person is saying.

3. Share yourself.

   Your enthusiasm, your genuine feelings about your church, and the difference your faith makes in your life.

4. If appropriate, agree on future steps for yourself and for those on whom you are calling.

After the call:

1. Make a note of all the information you have gathered: about concerns, frustrations, gripes expressed about groups or activities they should be invited to join; about the follow-up work from the church that is needed.
2. Tell each other how effective you were on the call and how you might improve the next one.

LET'S PRACTICE:

Step 1. Team of two volunteers to make practice call

Another team of two volunteers to role-play the kind of family that might be called on.

Third team agrees to observe and provide feedback.

Step 2. Callers agree on a plan of action.

Role players work out roles they will play.

Names

Family situation

Attitude toward your church and why?

Observers review "Suggestions for Callers"

Step 3. The call is made (no more than 10 minutes will be allowed).

Observers watch silently and take notes.

behaviors that seem to be helpful

behaviors that seem to block effective dialogue

Step 4. Group reflects on role-play experience.

How did callers and role players feel?

What helpful and/or hindering behaviors did observers see?

How could the call be improved?

Step 5. Repeat steps 1-4 with a new couple in each role.

Bibliography

Alves, Rubem. *Tomorrow's Child.* New York: Harper & Row, 1972.

Anastasia, A., W. Cohen and D.A. Spatz. "A Study of Fear and Anger in College Students Through the Controlled Diary Method," *Journal of General Psychology,* Vol. 73, 1948.

Argyle, Michael. *Religious Behavior.* London: Rootledge and Kegan Paul, 1958.

Bandura, Albert. *Aggression: A Social Learning Analysis.* Englewood Cliffs, N.J.: Prentice Hall, 1973.

Barbour, Ian G. *Issues in Science and Religion.* New York: Harper & Row, 1971.

Bowlby, John. "Processes of Mourning," *International Journal of Psychoanalysis,* Vol. 62, 1961.

Bretall, Robert (ed.). *A Kierkegaard Anthology.* Princeton: Princeton University Press, 1947.

Brewer, Earl D. D. and Associates. *Protestant Parish.* Atlanta: Communicative Arts Press, 1967.

Campbell, Thomas C., and Yoshio Fukuyama. *The Fragmented Layman.* Philadelphia: Unted Church Press, 1970.

Cauthen, Kenneth. *Science, Secularization, and God.* New York: Abingdon Press, 1969.

Chessick, Richard D., M.D. *How Psychotherapy Heals.* New York: Science House, Inc., 1969.

_____. *Technique and Practice of Intensive Psychotherapy.* New York: Jason Aronson, Inc., 1974.

Clinebell, Howard J., Jr. *Basic Types of Pastoral Counseling.* New York: Abingdon Press, 1966.

Coleman, John R. *Blue-Collar Journal: A College President's Sabbatical.* Philadelphia: J.B. Lippincott Company, 1974.

Committee on Medical Education. *Assessment of Sexual Function: A Guide to Interviewing.* New York: Jason Aronson, 1974.

Cox, Harvey. *The Secular City.* New York: The Macmillan Company, 1965.

_____. *The Seduction of the Spirit.* New York: Simon and Schuster, 1973.

Douglas, W. B., and M. Bloomfield. *Children Under Five.* Fair Lawn, N.J.: Essential Books, 1958.

Dustin, David S. *How Psychologists Do Research: The Example of Anxiety.* Englewood Cliffs, N.J.: Prentice-Hall, Inc., 1969.

Engel, George L., and Arthur H. Schmale. "Conversation-Withdrawal: A Primary Regulatory Process for Organismic Homeostasis," *Physiology, Emotion and Psychosomatic Illness,* 1972.

_____. "A Life Setting Conducive to Illness," *Annals of Internal Medicine*, Vol. 69, 1968.

_____. *Psychological Development in Health and Disease.* Philadelphia: W.B. Saunders Company, 1962.

Fichter, J.H. "The Profile of Catholic Religious Life," *American Journal of Sociology*, 58: 145-150, 1952.

Fischer, William F. *Theories of Anxiety.* New York: Harper & Row, 1970.

Frankl, Viktor E. *Man's Search for Meaning.* New York: Washington Square Press, Inc., 1964.

Fromm, Erich. *The Heart of Man: Its Genius for Good and Evil.* New York: Harper & Row, 1964.

Goldstein, K. "On Emotions," *Journal of Psychology*, XIX, 1951.

Greenwald, Harold (ed.). *Active Psychotherapy.* New York: Jason Aronson, 1974.

Haimowitz, Morris L. and Natalie Leader Haimowitz (eds.) *Human Development.* New York: Thomas Y. Crowell Company, 1960.

Hall, Calvin S., and Gardner Lindzey. *Theories of Personality.* (2nd Ed.). New York: John Wiley and Sons, Inc., 1970.

Hardon, John A., S.J. *The Protestant Churches of America.* Westminster, Md.: The Newman Press, 1962.

Harper, Robert A. *Psychoanalysis and Psychotherapy.* New York: Jason Aronson, 1974.

Harris, Thomas A., M.D. *I'm OK — You're OK.* New York: Harper & Row, 1969.

Heidegger, M. *Being and Time.* New York: Harper & Row, 1963.

Henry, Jules. *Pathways to Madness.* New York: Random House, 1971.

Hiltner, Seward. *Ferment in the Ministry.* New York: Abington Press, 1969.

Hiltner, Seward and Karl Menninger (eds.). *Constructive Aspects of Anxiety.* New York: Abington Press, 1963.

Holmes, Urban T., III. *The Future Shape of Ministry.* New York: The Seabury Press, 1971.

Jacquet, Constant H., Jr. (ed.). *Yearbook of American and Canadian Churches, 1974.* Nashville: Abingdon Press, 1974.

Johnson, Douglas W., and others. *Churches and Church Membership in the United States.* Washington, D.C.: Glenmary Research Center, 1971.

Johnson, Douglas W., and George W. Cornell. *Punctured Preconceptions.* New York. Friendship Press, 1972.

Jourard, Sidney. *Self-disclosure.* New York: Wiley Interscience, 1971.

_____. *The Transparent Self.* New York: Van Norstrand Reinhold, 1971.

Jud, Gerald J., and Associates. *Ex-Pastors: Why Men Leave the Parish Ministry.* Philadelphia: Pilgrim Press, 1970.

Lader, M.H. (ed.). "Studies of Anxiety," *British Journal of Psychiatric Special Publication No. 3*. Asford, Kent: Headley Brothers, Ltd., 1967.

Leiffer, Murray H. *Changing Expectations and Ethics in the Professional Ministry*. Evanston, Ill.: Murray H. Leiffer, 1969.

Lewis, G. Douglass (ed.). *Explorations in Ministry*. New York: IDOC, North America, 1971.

Lidz, Theodore. *The Person*. New York: Basic Books, Inc., 1968.

Lowrie, Walter (trans.). *The Concept of Dread*, by Soren Kierkegaard. Princeton: Princeton University Press, 1944.

Mager, Robert F. *Goal Analysis*. Belmont: Lear Siegler, Inc./Fearon Publishers, 1972.

Menninger, Karl. *The Vital Balance*. New York: The Viking Press, 1963.

Merton, P. Strommen and Associates. *A Study of Generations*. Minneapolis: Augsburg Publishing House, 1972.

Miller, Derek. *Adolescence: Psychology, Psychopathology, and Psychotherapy*. New York: Jason Aronson, 1974.

Niebuhr, Reinhold. *The Nature and Destiny of Man: A Christian Interpretation*. New York: Scharles Scribner & Sons, 1941.

Oates, Wayne E. *The Psychology of Religion*. Waco: Word Books, 1973.

Parkes, Murray. "Separation Anxiety: An Aspect of the Search of a Lost Object," *British Journal of Psychiatry Special Publication No. 3*, ed. M.H. Lader, Ashford, Kent: Headley Brothers, Ltd., 1967.

Parsegian, V.L. *This Cybernetic World of Men, Machines, and Earth Systems*. Garden City: Doubleday & Company, Inc., 1973.

Peterson, W.F. *Man—Weather—Sun*. Springfield: Charles C. Thomas, 1948.

Powys, John Cowper. *The Meaning of Culture*. New York: Norton, 1929.

Pressey, Sidney L., and Raymond Kuhlen. *Psychological Development Through the Life Span*. New York: Harper and Brothers, 1957.

Ramsey, Paul. *Fabricated Man*. New Haven: Yale University Press, 1970.

Reik, T. *Listening with the Third Ear*. New York: Pyramid Publications, 1972.

Rogers, Carl. *Carl Rogers on Encounter Groups*. New York: Harper & Row, 1970.

Rubin, Theodore Isaac, M.D. *The Angry Book*. New York: Collier Books, 1969.

Saltzman, M. *Clinical Audiology*. New York: Grune P. Stratton, 1949.

Schaller, Lyle E. *The Pastor and the People*. Nashville: Abingdon Press, 1973.

Schmale, Arthur H., Jr. "A Genetic View of Affects," *The Psychoanalytical Study of the Child*, Vol. XIX, 1964.

Schmale, Arthur H. Jr., and George L. Engel. "The Giving Up—Given Up Complex," *Arch. Gen. Psychiatry*, Vol. 17, August, 1967.

Schmale, Arthur H. Jr., and others. "Experimental Induction of Affects," *ACTA Medica Psychosomatica*, Rome, September, 1967.

Schmale, A.H. "Giving Up as a Final Common Pathway to Changes in Health," *Adv. Psychosomatic Medicine*, Vol. 8, 1973.

Stark, Rodney, and Charles Y. Glock. *American Piety: The Nature of Religious Commitment*. Los Angeles: University of California Press, 1968.

Sterns, Frederic R. *Anger: Psychology, Physiology, Pathology*. Springfield: Charles C. Thomas, 1972.

Sullivan, Harvey Stack. *The Psychiatric Interview*. New York: W.W. Horton and Co., Inc., 1970.

Thornton, Edward E. *Theology and Pastoral Counseling*. Philadelphia: Fortress Press, 1964.

Tillich, Paul. *The Courage To Be*. New Haven: Yale University Press, 1956.

_____. *Systematic Theology*, Vol. II. Chicago: University of Chicago Press, 1957.

Williamson, Donald S. "A Study of Selective Inhibition of Aggression by Church Members," *The Journal of Pastoral Care*, Vol. XXI, December, 1967.

Wolf, Anna W.M. *Insights: A Selection of Creative Literature About Children*. New York: Jason Aronson, 1973.

Young, P.T. "Laughing and Weeping, Cheerfulness and Depression. A Study of Moods Among College Students," *Journal of Social Psychology*, Vol. 8, 1937.

Subject Index

church members, with,
45, 46, 52, 53, 56, 66-68, 83,
93-97;
education, over, 45-47, 52,
54, 93-95;
family, with, 11, 41, 45, 46,
52, 53, 56, 66-68, 85, 93, 94,
96, 97;
financial, 11, 41, 45, 46, 52,
53, 56, 66-68, 85, 93, 94,
96, 97;
moral values, over, 45, 46;
pastor, with, 45, 52, 53, 56,
66-68, 83, 93, 94, 96, 97;
theological values, over,
11, 45, 46, 52, 59, 93, 95
"Conservation-withdrawal,"
31, 35, 57
Contract, the training, 73
Cornell, George W., 14, 33
Counter-transference, 71, 82
Cousins, Norman, 32
Courage, 18
Creativity, 4, 19-21, 24, 58,
61, 63
Crying, 17, 57, 83
Data, 11, 36-54;
sample defined, 36-37;
return rate, 36-37;
comparison of groupings,
38-54;
sociological, 38-41;
behavioral, 41-45;
precipitate, 45-47, 93;
summary, 52-54
Davis, Angela, 15
Death, 18, 23, 45;
(See also nonbeing)
Delusion, 5
Denial, 8
Depression, 4, 23, 26, 86;
-withdrawal, 6
Design of investigation, 8, 9
Despair, 29, 65
Development, 18

Diagnosis, 85-87;
of apathetic, 85;
of bored, 86;
of helpless, 85;
of undifferentiated, 86, 87
Disequilibrium, 5, 17
Disinterested members
(See apathy, boredom)
Displacement, 4, 27
Displeasure, 5
Divorce, 45
"Dizziness," 20, 61
Douglas, W. B., 17, 33
"Dread," 34
"Dreaming innocence," 22
Dropout problem, 12, 14, 52-54
Dropout tracks, 68, 69
Drugs, 4, 26
Dustin, David S., 33
Eby, L., 35
Education;
conflict, 45-47, 52, 54, 93-95;
level of, 8, 40, 45, 46, 52, 54,
95
Energy of anxiety, 19, 58
Engel, George L., 10, 12, 27,
31, 35
Environment, 6, 18, 28, 62, 63,
65, 68
Erikson, 30, 63
Equilibrium, 3, 17, 56, 63;
(See also disequilibrium)
Evangelical United Brethren,
13
Evangelism, 73
Evil, 20
Exhaustion, 6
Existential anxiety, 4, 5, 56,
68, 97
"Existential vacuum," 31
Existentialism, 19
Expected success, 4
Faith;
articulation of, 41, 44, 45, 52,
53, 59, 85, 93, 94;

139

Tension, 17, 18;
  psychic, 3
"Threat of nothingness," 7
Theology, 11, 54;
  dynamics of, 11, 54;
  framework, as, 3
Theological values, conflict
  over, 11, 45, 46, 52, 59, 86,
  93, 95
Thurston's Personality
  Schedule, 16
Tillich, Paul, 5, 7, 12, 19, 22,
  23, 34
Tinling, D., 35
Tiredness and anger, 25
Touch and anger, 25
Training;
  clergy, 77-79;
  contract, 73;
  function, 72;
  interviewers, 10, 37, 38,
  92, 93;
  laity, 79-80;
  methodology, 72-77, 92, 93;
  recruitment, 10, 37, 38, 73

Transcendence, 21
Transference, 82;
  (See also counter-
  transference)
Trust, 30, 84
Uneasiness, 3, 5
United Methodist Church, 13
United Presbyterian Church,
  15
Unworthiness, 63, 82
Violence, 4
Visitation, 72-89
Williamson, Donald S., 71
Young, P. T., 34
Withdrawal, 4, 6, 23, 31, 35,
  57, 63, 65, 86
Worship, 2;
  attitude towards, 84;
  habits, 93, 94;
  (See also attendance)

DATE DUE
